T0194956

Fig Tree Planner

John Gonzalez

WESTBOW
PRESS®
A DIVISION OF THOMAS NELSON
& ZONDERVAN

WestBow Press books may be ordered through booksellers or by contacting:

WestBow Press
A Division of Thomas Nelson & Zondervan
1663 Liberty Drive
Bloomington, IN 47403
www.westbowpress.com
844-714-3454

Because of the dynamic nature of the Internet, any web addresses or links contained in this book may have changed since publication and may no longer be valid. The views expressed in this work are solely those of the author and do not necessarily reflect the views of the publisher, and the publisher hereby disclaims any responsibility for them.

Any people depicted in stock imagery provided by Getty Images are models, and such images are being used for illustrative purposes only. Certain stock imagery © Getty Images.

ISBN: 978-1-6642-3866-4 (sc)
ISBN: 978-1-6642-3865-7 (hc)
ISBN: 978-1-6642-3867-1 (e)

Library of Congress Control Number: 2021913185

Print information available on the last page.

WestBow Press rev. date: 7/13/2021

"If you want to reach your goals and fulfill your potential, become intentional about your personal growth. It will change your life!"
– John C. Maxwell

Introduction

Fig Tree Planner is designed to help you form a deliberate, trackable process by structuring daily life and working on annual goals. It gives the ability to be more intentional daily and partners with you on achieving goals throughout the year. We walk with you from marking out an annual larger goal that can seem intimidating and break that down into bite-sized portions daily with stopping points to look at progress and fine-tune any areas that are not lining up with the overall goals.

We want to help people discover what is important and a lifestyle that helps them attain a more intentional peace-filled life!

I have been fortunate to have the opportunity to counsel and help people overcome and succeed in their lives. It was a very rewarding but also challenging process at times, not so much because the people lacked the desire to succeed but lacked the organizational and time-management skills. I would often instruct them on certain actions that were urgent for them to execute change in their lives. When I later checked on their progress, their responses for not taking action were often "I didn't have time," "I forgot," "I did it for only a few days," "I just didn't know where to start," "I don't know how," "I lost my motivation," and so on.

I could often relate to them because I too had to overcome the same challenges at one time. This planner is the result of much research and personal experience. I have taken proven and highly effective strategies used by very successful people and organized them in a simple, easy-to-understand, inspirational planner that will keep you focused, organized, motivated, and on track throughout the year. This planner is designed to help you close the gap between where you are and where you want to be!

What is a Morning Routine

Having a morning routine is extremely important. Most successful people throughout history have had morning routines. They enable you to set up your day and life for success. Most people don't have a morning routine and thus wake up feeling tired and unmotivated. Why? Because they are being reactive rather than proactive.

Having a morning routine causes you to be proactive and can change your life in all areas, such as body, health, productivity, spirituality, finances, and relationships.

Deep Breathing

Engaging in deep breathing is one of the quickest ways to become calm and energized. Deep breathing improves the function of many of your body's systems, including your nervous system, immune system, digestive system, respiratory system, and lymphatic system.

Wake up in the morning and take some long and very deep breaths, holding three to five seconds and breathing out slowly.

Hydration

Water is an essential ingredient of all living things. Is 70 percent of the human body comprised of water? The average person loses about two and a half liters of fluid throughout the day. One of the best things that you can do when you wake up in the morning is hydrate yourself. Your body becomes dehydrated while you sleep. Drinking water right after you wake up will rehydrate you, boost your body's metabolism, and help your body flush out toxins. It also increases the blood flow to your brain, giving you the energy to conquer your day.

Exercise

One of the biggest secrets to having energy all day is exercise in the morning. Exercise ignites your metabolism. Regardless of your age or fitness level, studies show that making exercise a part of your daily routine does everything from cutting cancer and stroke risk to building stronger muscles and bones, alleviating anxiety and depression, and encouraging better brain health and digestion.

Claude Bouchard, the director of human genomics at the Pennington Biomedical Research Center in Louisiana, said, "There is no pill that comes close to what exercise can do." It is possible to form a positive addiction to exercise for a lifetime.

Decrees / Affirmations

The word "decree" can be defined as:

- ○ an authoritative instruction provided by someone who has authority or by a government, or

- ○ a judgment decided by a court of law.

And so the tongue is a small part of the body yet it carries great power! Just think of how a small flame can set a huge forest ablaze. And the tongue is a fire! It can be compared to the sum total of wickedness and is the most dangerous part of our human body. It corrupts the entire body and is a hellish flame! It releases a fire that can burn throughout the course of human existence.

Every wild animal on earth, including birds, creeping reptiles, and creatures of the sea and land, has been overpowered and tamed by humans, but the tongue is not able to be tamed. It can be a fickle, unrestrained evil that spews out words full of poison! We use our tongue to praise God our Father and then turn around and curse a person who was made in His very image!

From the same mouth, we pour out words of praise one minute and curses the next. My brothers and sisters, this should never be! (James 3:5–10)

The above scripture demonstrates the power of our words, but even more powerful is when we make spiritual proclamations that come from God Himself (from His Word). Jesus said that His words are spirit and life. They are filled with power, so proclaiming God's words in faith activates His will and purpose for your life.

For we have the living Word of God, which is full of energy, and it pierces more sharply than a two-edged sword. It will even penetrate to the very core of our being where soul and spirit, bone and marrow meet! It interprets and reveals the true thoughts and secret motives of our hearts. (Hebrews 4:12)

Thou shalt also decree a thing, and it shall be established unto thee: and the light shall shine upon thy ways. (Job 22:28)

An additional benefit of proclaiming the Word of God is that your mind is renewed to who you are in Christ, which is a loved child of God designed to have abundant life!

Some sample decrees:

"My God meets all my needs according to His riches in glory by Christ."

"The Lord makes me abound in prosperity."

"My family is walking in the light of God's love, and all dark schemes of the enemy will be utterly thwarted."

"I am strong and courageous, and I encourage those surrounding me to be strong and courageous."

Show Gratitude

Do you want more from your life? More happiness? Better health? Deeper relationships? Increased productivity?

Scripture instructs us to be thankful to God every day for everything.

Have you ever heard the phrase "count your blessings"? When you start your day by being thankful to God for what you have and what He has given you, instead of dwelling on what is missing you will train yourself to focus on the good and more good things will be given to you. The list of things we could praise Him for is endless.

Scientific research proves scripture and reveals that expressing gratitude may be one of the simplest ways to feel better, and it also helps in improving physical and psychological health.

There is a human trait called hedonic adaptation. Which means that we get used to the good things that happen to us after repeated exposure. We also get used to the bad things that happen to us.

For example: If someone gets into a car accident and is disabled, hedonic adaptation causes them to eventually get used to and adapt to their disability and soon they can be just as happy as the rest of us. Hedonic adaptation gives unparalleled resiliency and keeps us motivated to achieve even greater things. It can also destroy certain good things in our lives such as our marriages – we get used to our amazing spouse (or children, or job, or house, or car). We start complaining about things and people we previously thought of as positives in our lives.

We must consciously and intentionally fight hedonic adaptation in order to maximize happiness. Gratitude is one of the most powerful tools in our arsenal because it helps remind us of the good things that are already in our lives.

Studies show that gratitude makes us feel more gratitude. It is a positivity loop that increases this feeling over time.

Write down at least 3 things that you are grateful to God for every morning.

Consider the following scriptures:

Psalm 100:4 *"Enter his gates **with Thanksgiving** and his courts with praise; give thanks to him and praise His name".*

Psalm 95:2-3 *"Let us come before him **with Thanksgiving** and extol him with music and song. For the Lord is the great God, the great king above all gods".*

1 Chronicles 16:34 *"**Give thanks** to the Lord, for he is good...".*

Psalm 106:1 *"Praise the Lord. **Give thanks** to the Lord for he is good; his love endures forever"*

Psalm 107:15 *"Let them **give thanks** to the Lord for his unfailing love and his wonderful deeds for mankind...".*

Psalm 28:7 *"The Lord is my strength and my shield; my heart trusts in him and he helps me. My heart leaps for joy and with my song **I praise him**".*

Daniel 2:23 *"**I thank** and praise you, God of my ancestors: you have given me wisdom and power...".*

Philippians 4:6 *"Do not be anxious about anything, but by prayer and petition, **with thanksgiving**, present your requests to God".*

Ephesians 5:19-20 *"Sing and make music from your heart to the Lord, always giving thanks to God the Father for everything, in the name of our Lord Jesus Christ".*

In what situation has God provided for you?

Isaiah 12:1 *"**I will praise you**, Lord. Although you were angry with me, your anger has turned away and you have comforted me".*

Psalm 103:2-3 *"**Praise the Lord**, my soul, and forget not all his benefits - who forgives all your sins...".*

What sins has God forgiven you for?

Colossians 3:16 *"Let the message of Christ dwell among you richly as you teach and admonish one another with all wisdom through psalms, hymns, and songs from the Spirit, singing to God **with gratitude** in your hearts".*

Psalm 119:62 *"At midnight I rise to **give you thanks** for your righteous laws"*.

What Bible verse has made a difference in your faith walk?

Psalm 136:3-9 "**Give thanks** to the Lord of lords: to him who alone does great wonders, who by his understanding made the heavens, who spread out the earth upon the waters, who made the great lights - the sun to govern the day, the moon and stars to govern the night...".

1 Thessalonians 1:2 "We always **thank God** for all of you and continually mention you in our prayers".

Philemon 1:4 "I **always thank** my God as I remember you in my prayers, because I hear about your love for all his holy people and their faith in the Lord Jesus".

2 Thessalonians 1:3 "We ought **always to thank** God for you, brothers and sisters, and rightly so, because your face is growing more and more and the love all of you have for one another is increasing".

How has being part of God's family with your Christian brothers and sisters made a difference in how you live?

2 Corinthians 2:14 "But thanks be to God, who always leads us as captives in Christ's triumphal procession and uses us to spread the aroma of the knowledge of him everywhere".

1 Corinthians 15:57 "But thanks be to God! He gives us the victory through our Lord Jesus Christ" .

Hebrews 12:28-29 Therefore, since we are receiving a kingdom that cannot be shaken, let us be thankful, and so worship God acceptably with reverence and awe, for our 'God is a consuming fire".

Revelation 11:17 "We give thanks to you, Lord God Almighty, the One who is and who was, because you have taken your great power and have begun to reign".

How has the knowledge of God's plan for you now and in the future encouraged you?

Giving thanks every day to God will bring us to a place of humility, and a place of joy, and that is how God wants us to live every day.

Psalm 116:12-14 "What shall I return to the Lord for all his goodness to me? I will lift up the cup of salvation and call on the name of the Lord. I will fulfill my vows to the Lord in the presence of all his people".

Pray / Meditate

James 5:16-18 *tells us "for tremendous power is released through the passionate, heartfelt prayer of a godly believer!"* Prayer is how we communicate with God.

Why is it a good idea to communicate with God on a daily basis?

Because God wants to partner with you to accomplish His will for your life. The power of prayer should never be underestimated because it draws on the power and might of the infinitely powerful God of the Universe.

Praying is asking God for His help.

Psalm 107:28–30 states,

Then we cried out, "Lord, help us! Rescue us!" And he did! God stilled the storm, calmed the waves, and he hushed the hurricane winds to only a whisper. We were so relieved, so glad as he guided us safely to harbor in a quiet haven.

The Bible tells us that we can ask God for help for anything and everything. Philippians 4:6–7 says,

Don't be pulled in different directions or worried about a thing. Be saturated in prayer throughout each day, offering your faith-filled requests before God with overflowing gratitude. Tell him every detail of your life, then God's wonderful peace that transcends human understanding, will make the answers known to you through Jesus Christ.

There is no doubt that prayer is effective.

The Bible gives us accounts of prayer defeating enemies (Psalm 6:9–10), defeating death (2 Kings 4:3–36), healing sickness and disease (James 5:14–15), and conquering demons (Mark 9:29). As an answer to prayer, God heals wounds, opens eyes, transforms hearts, heals wounds, and gives wisdom.

Anytime is a good time to pray.

I have found that in my life, early morning prayer is the best time to pray. Jesus prayed in the morning (Mark 1:35). The next morning, Jesus got up long before daylight, left the house while it was dark, and made His way to a secluded place to give Himself to prayer. I believe God wants to hear from us first thing in the morning because it's the perfect time for God to give us instructions for the day.

Make it your personal goal to use the morning routine to start your day with prayer.

Plan Your Day

Use the weekly planner and to-do lists to plan your day. In order to develop a highly effective day and make progress in achieving your goals, you must plan your day. Planning requires self-discipline and commitment, but Fig Tree Planner is the perfect tool for the job.

You should have already created your list of weekly tasks at the beginning of the week. Now use that to plan your day. Take a few tasks from each area of your life and list them in your to-do list, then prioritize them in order of execution.

In the words of Stephen Keague, "Proper planning and preparation prevents poor performance."

Annual Goals Explained

Goal Areas

These are the areas of your life. Pick the top areas of your life you want to focus on to achieve certain goals in your life this year. You can also pick a project as one of your categories. For instance, if you are getting married this year or you have a graduation party to plan then this would be a goal area for this year or quarter.

Possible Goal Areas:

1. Health//Fitness

2. Mind Growth

3. Emotional Control / Manage

4. Relationships

5. Mission & Purpose

6. Finances / Money

7. Family & Friends

8. Spirituality

9. Charity / helping others

10. Fun

11. Home / Personal / Household

Results

List the end result you want to achieve. For instance, if your goal area is health and fitness, then a result could be to lose thirty pounds this year. Use the SMART.

SMART stands for:

○ Specific – Clarity is power

○ Measurable – Keeps you on track seeing where you are at all times

○ Attainable & Realistic – Your goal must convince your mind that it is possible

○ Timeline – Set a deadline for your goal, typically one year.

*Creating SMART results is very powerful because it causes you to gain small victories which changes your psyche and strengthens your commitment.

Results

This is your why. For example, why do you want to connect with God? Your whys could be to avoid pain (i.e., "I don't want to miss what God has planned for me.") or to gain pleasure (i.e., "I want to hear God say 'Well done, good and faithful servant.'") List at least three reasons why you want to achieve your goal.

These whys will anchor you by reminding you every day why you are dedicated to achieving this goal.

Annual Goals Example

The Lord directs the steps of the godly. He delights in every detail of their lives. Though they stumble, they will never fall, for the Lord holds them by the hand.
——Psalm 37:23–24

Goal Area:

Business

Detailed Desired Result:

I will launch my online business this year!

I will make at least $1,000 / month!

Purpose:

-To earn more money for myself / my family.

-To gain more freedom in my life

-To finally pursue my passion

Goal Area:

Mind / Beliefs

Detailed Desired Result:

I will get rid of limiting beliefs!

I will get rid of negativity!

I will improve my intellect!

Purpose:

-To better understand life

-To gain influence

-To achieve my goals in life

-To be more positive/peaceful

Goal Area:

Health / Fitness

Detailed Desired Result:

I will easily improve my eating habits!

I will lose thirty pounds of fat!

Purpose:

-To have more energy

-To look good and have more confidence

-To live a healthier and longer life

Goal Area:

Relationships

Detailed Desired Result:

I will connect and be more intimate with my family and friends!

I will eliminate toxic relationships!

Purpose:

-To enrich my life with people who build me up

-To enrich my life by building others up

-To cherish those who are important to me

-To feel inspired, fulfilled, joyous, and happy

Annual Goals Example

Commit to the Lord whatever you do, and he will establish your plans.
——Proverbs 16:3

Goal Area:

Spiritual

Detailed Desired Result:

I will read through the entire Bible and
one spiritual book this year!

Purpose:

- To better understand spiritual things.
- To connect with my creator.
- To discover my destiny.

Goal Area:

Project: Family Trip to Italy

Detailed Desired Result:

I will take my family on a once and a
lifetime trip to Italy full of fun and
relaxation!

Purpose:

-To make my family happy.
-To experience the joy of travel.
-To have a unique bonding experience
with my family.

Goal Area:

Emotions

Detailed Desired Result:

I will learn and practice emotional
intelligence!

Purpose:

-To feel great.
-To control my emotions and not allow
my emotions to control me.
To not make emotional decisions.

Goal Area:

Fun

Detailed Desired Result:

I will plan at least two to three fun
events every week with my family or
friends!

Purpose:

-To enjoy my life's journey.
-To relieve stress.
-To become a fun person.

Weekly Goal Strategies Example

Goal Area: Business

- Make a list of things I like to do.
- Ask family / friends what I am good at
- Start looking for online classes.
- Start separate savings account for business / training centered expenses.
- Start creating list of possible business names.
- Look for mentornames.

Goal Area: Health / Fitness

- Join gym.
- Research eating plans.
- Research best books on health and fitness.
- Get a physical.
- Make list of possible accountability partners

Goal Area: Mind / Beliefs

- Make list of my limiting beliefs.
- Research books about Overcoming.
- Research how to improve my thinking
- Find daily affirmations that apply to overcoming limiting beliefs.

Goal Area: Relationships

- Send email to Brian.
- Make list of people that I want to have bigger priority in my life.
- List of people I need to ask forgiveness from.
- List people that are toxic to my life and well being.
- Find Relationship building books.

Weekly Goal Strategies Example

Week of: April 19-25

Goal Area: Spiritual

- Buy One Year Reading Bible.
- Research book about prayer / meditation.
- Make list of possible churches to try.
- Start reading Bible and taking notes.
- Research best books for spiritual enlightenment.

Goal Area: Emotions

- Start formulating plan for emotional stability.
- Buy book about emotional intelligence.
- Make list of my toxic emotions.
- Research how to keep my emotions in peak state at all times.

Goal Area: Family Trip to Italy

- Start researching dates and ticket prices.
- Open up separate savings account.
- Get everyone passports.

Goal Area: Fun

- Make list of fun things to do.
- Invite Mark to concert.
- Make list of free fun things (helps with saving money).

Morning Routine Example

This is the Day the Lord has made, I will rejoice and be glad in it!
——Psalm 118:24

MORNING ROUTINE

DECREES / AFFIRMATION:

- Discouragement flees from me because God grants me endurance and encouragement!
- I am blessed with a bright future that is full of hope and joyful expectation for an awesome outcome!
- I am blessed beyond all I am able to ask, think or imagine!

THINGS I AM THANKFUL TO GOD FOR TODAY:

1. For Jesus and the gift of salvation
2. My family
3. My health

TYPE OF EXERCISE

Bench press

Triceps

Biceps

Sit up / Crunches

Run (Treadmill)

AMOUNT (DISTANCE, TIME, SETS, REPS, WEIGHT)

200 lbs : 3 sets of 10

60 lbs : 3 sets of 10

45 lbs : 3 sets of 10

3 sets of 30

Level 8 : 30 mins

CUPS OF WATER: ⬧ ⬧ ⬧ ⬧ ⬧ ⬧ ⬧ ⬧

BREATHING EXERCISE: ✓

PRAYER \ MEDITATION \ READING NOTES

Reading the word in Isaiah vs 35:4 it really spoke to me. It says to those with fearful hearts "be strong, do not fear your God will come, He will come with vengeance ; with divine retribution, He will come to save you"

I believe God is telling me that He defends and protects me.
He will save me from my spiritual enemies and my worldly enemies.
I am so thankful for His comforting words!

NOTES / APPOINTMENTS FOR THE DAY:
-Dr. Appt today
-Teacher meeting for Jimmy @ 2p
- Don't forget to pick up dry cleaning!

Quarterly Goal Evaluation Example

o How did I do at working towards my goal this quarter?
o What things should I start doing to reach my goal?
o What things should I stop doing that are holding me back?
o What should I keep doing that has/have been helping?
o Prayer Requests / Answered Prayers

GOAL — Business

o I made progress. I identified that I want to start a digital marketing business. I have a few online learning classes I will be starting soon to help me brush up on my skills.
o I will start all the necessary steps to become a legitimate business and start some small projects from people I know in the community that want some work done for their business websites.
o I will stop allowing doubt into my mind. I will no longer let my insecurities hold me back.
o I will keep reaching out to others I know who have started their own businesses for support.
o God, I know this is what You have told me to do. Continue to give me direction and confidence!

GOAL — Health / Fitness

o I have not consistently been working out. I have been eating much healthier though!
o I will make sure to start trying to have the whole family go with me so I am sure to go more often.
o I will stop allowing myself to spiral into guilt of not making the progress I want. This only makes me continue the trend to not work out.
o I will keep eating well by cooking at home more. I have been eating out less (saving money), and it helps me make better, more deliberate food choices!
o I will ask God to help me remove false definers. I am a finisher even if I don't feel that way.

GOAL — Mind / Beliefs

o I am trying to identify my beliefs and areas in my life that try to hinder them. It has been very eye-opening and has helped my family do the same.
o I will start sharing this process with my closest friends so they can help me and maybe do the same so we can do it together with our families.
o I need to stop allowing other people's beliefs cloud my own!
o The daily affirmations have been a big part of helping me know my beliefs and stand by them as daily reminders!
o God, help me see the parts of my life I need to change because they don't go along with my personal beliefs.

GOAL — Relationships

o This is one goal I have had the most progress in. I have looked deeply at my relationships and have been able to identify the important ones.
o I will start creating more space for my important relationships on a weekly basis.
o I will stop feeling guilty when I know someone is no longer supposed to have the priority in my life they held in the past!
o I will keep telling those who are important to me how much they mean to me and why!
o I am so thankful that God has been showing me who to invest my time in and who not. It brings peace and more joy!

16

Let God transform you into a new person by changing the way you think, then you will learn to know God's will for you which is good and pleasing and perfect.
------Romans 12:2 (NLT)

GOAL

Spiritual

o I have visited a couple churches and am liking one I have been to two times (not consistently) so far, and I have been reading One Year Reading Bible.
o I will start going to this church consistently and continue asking God if I belong there. o I will stop finding excuses not to go to church.
o Reading the Bible daily has really helped me put more priority in God and my search for a church.
o God, help me find the church You have called me to!

GOAL

Emotions

o Making this a goal has made me more able to see my reactions out of emotions in almost every situation, which has in turn caused me to be more careful how I respond, before I respond.
o I will start reading my new book I bought weeks ago on the importance of emotional health.
o I will stop allowing my emotions to negatively affect myself or others!
o I will keep making myself take a breath in before responding in situations. This is helping me have the time to choose a correct response not out of emotions.
o God has helped me feel more at peace when I chose the correct response. He is with me on this!

GOAL

Family Trip to Italy

o I have made good progress on this. I have the entire family involved on reaching and planning ideas to save money or places we want to see.
o I will start saving a little more each check.
o I will stop spending money on eating out and reduce drinking coffee in shops to help save more money.
o Having the entire family involved helps me be more deliberate with this goal in making sure it happens!
o God, help this not only be fun and a new experience but help it be an investment in our family relationship.

GOAL

Fun

o This goal has touched my other goals of relationships, health, and fitness by doing more fun activities with people who are important to me and things that are outdoors, which usually is good for health and fitness too.
o I will start learning new hobbies that are fun and can ask a friend to learn with me.
o I will stop allowing lack of time to hinder this. I can have fun with the family doing daily things.
o What has helped is joining it with my other goals. This makes me feel more productive and happier.
o God, help me to continue this so that I have increased joy in my life.

Annual Goals

The Lord directs the steps of the godly. He delights in every detail of their lives. Though they stumble, they will never fall, for the Lord holds them by the hand.
—Psalm 37:23–24

Goal Area: Goal Area:

Detailed Desired Result: Detailed Desired Result:

_____   _____
_____   _____
_____   _____

Purpose: Purpose:

_____   _____
_____   _____

Goal Area: Goal Area:

Detailed Desired Result: Detailed Desired Result:

_____   _____
_____   _____
_____   _____

Purpose: Purpose:

_____   _____
_____   _____

Annual Goals

The Lord directs the steps of the godly. He delights in every detail of their lives. Though
they stumble, they will never fall, for the Lord holds them by the hand.
—Psalm 37:23–24

Goal Area: Goal Area:

Detailed Desired Result: Detailed Desired Result:

Purpose: Purpose:

Goal Area: Goal Area:

Detailed Desired Result: Detailed Desired Result:

Purpose: Purpose:

Month:

SUNDAY	MONDAY	TUESDAY	WEDNESDAY

THURSDAY	FRIDAY	SATURDAY	NOTES

Weekly Goal Strategies

Goal Area: ....

_____
_____
_____
_____
_____
_____
_____
_____
_____
_____
_____
_____
_____
_____

Goal Area: ....

_____
_____
_____
_____
_____
_____
_____
_____
_____
_____
_____
_____

Goal Area: ....

_____
_____
_____
_____
_____
_____
_____
_____
_____
_____
_____
_____

Goal Area: ....

_____
_____
_____
_____
_____
_____
_____
_____
_____
_____
_____
_____
_____

Weekly Goal Strategies

Goal Area:

_____
_____
_____
_____
_____
_____
_____
_____
_____
_____
_____
_____

Goal Area:

_____
_____
_____
_____
_____
_____
_____
_____
_____
_____
_____

Goal Area:

_____
_____
_____
_____
_____
_____
_____
_____
_____
_____
_____

Goal Area:

_____
_____
_____
_____
_____
_____
_____
_____
_____
_____
_____
_____
_____

Sunday

This is the Day the Lord has made, I will rejoice and be glad in it!
—Psalm 118:24

MORNING ROUTINE

DECREES / AFFIRMATION:

THINGS I AM THANKFUL TO GOD FOR TODAY:

1.
2.
3.

TYPE OF EXERCISE

AMOUNT (DISTANCE, TIME, SETS, REPS, WEIGHT)

CUPS OF WATER: ⬡⬡⬡⬡⬡⬡⬡   BREATHING EXERCISE:

PRAYER \ MEDITATION \ READING NOTES

NOTES / APPOINTMENTS FOR THE DAY:

Now Plan Your Day ☺

Monday

O God, you are my God early will I seek you.
-----Psalm 63:1

MORNING ROUTINE

DECREES / AFFIRMATION:

THINGS I AM THANKFUL TO GOD FOR TODAY:

1. _____
2. _____
3. _____

TYPE OF EXERCISE

AMOUNT (DISTANCE, TIME, SETS, REPS, WEIGHT)

_____

_____

_____

_____

CUPS OF WATER: ⬡⬡⬡⬡⬡⬡⬡   BREATHING EXERCISE: [____]

PRAYER \ MEDITATION \ READING NOTES

_____

_____

_____

_____

_____

_____

_____

NOTES / APPOINTMENTS FOR THE DAY:

Now Plan Your Day

Tuesday

In the morning, O Lord, you hear my voice; in the morning I will order my prayer to you and eagerly watch.
—Psalm 5:3

MORNING ROUTINE

DECREES / AFFIRMATION:

THINGS I AM THANKFUL TO GOD FOR TODAY:

1.
2.
3.

TYPE OF EXERCISE

AMOUNT (DISTANCE, TIME, SETS, REPS, WEIGHT)

CUPS OF WATER: ⬡⬡⬡⬡⬡⬡⬡⬡

BREATHING EXERCISE:

PRAYER \ MEDITATION \ READING NOTES

NOTES / APPOINTMENTS FOR THE DAY:

Now Plan Your Day ☺

Wednesday

Let me hear in the morning of your steadfast love, for in you I trust. Make me know the way I should go, for to you I lift up my soul.
—Psalm 143:8

MORNING ROUTINE

DECREES / AFFIRMATION:

THINGS I AM THANKFUL TO GOD FOR TODAY:

1. _____
2. _____
3. _____

TYPE OF EXERCISE

AMOUNT (DISTANCE, TIME, SETS, REPS, WEIGHT)

CUPS OF WATER: ⬡⬡⬡⬡⬡⬡⬡⬡

BREATHING EXERCISE: [ ]

PRAYER \ MEDITATION \ READING NOTES

NOTES / APPOINTMENTS FOR THE DAY:

Now Plan Your Day

Thursday

Take delight in the Lord, and He will give you your heart's desires. Commit everything you do to the Lord. Trust Him, and He will help you.
—Psalm 37:4–5

MORNING ROUTINE

DECREES / AFFIRMATION:

THINGS I AM THANKFUL TO GOD FOR TODAY:

1.
2.
3.

TYPE OF EXERCISE

AMOUNT (DISTANCE, TIME, SETS, REPS, WEIGHT)

CUPS OF WATER: ⬦⬦⬦⬦⬦⬦⬦

BREATHING EXERCISE:

PRAYER \ MEDITATION \ READING NOTES

NOTES / APPOINTMENTS FOR THE DAY:

Now Plan Your Day ☺

28

Friday

Give thanks in all circumstances; for this is the will of God in Christ Jesus for you.
—1 Thessalonians 5:18

MORNING ROUTINE

DECREES / AFFIRMATION:

THINGS I AM THANKFUL TO GOD FOR TODAY:

1. _____
2. _____
3. _____

TYPE OF EXERCISE

AMOUNT (DISTANCE, TIME, SETS, REPS, WEIGHT)

CUPS OF WATER: ⬦⬦⬦⬦⬦⬦⬦   BREATHING EXERCISE: [____]

PRAYER \ MEDITATION \ READING NOTES

NOTES / APPOINTMENTS FOR THE DAY:

Now Plan Your Day

Saturday

Because of the Lord's great love we are not consumed for his compassions never fail. They are new every morning, great is your faithfulness.
—Lamentations 3:22–23

MORNING ROUTINE

DECREES / AFFIRMATION:

THINGS I AM THANKFUL TO GOD FOR TODAY:

1.
2.
3.

TYPE OF EXERCISE

AMOUNT (DISTANCE, TIME, SETS, REPS, WEIGHT)

CUPS OF WATER: ⬡⬡⬡⬡⬡⬡⬡⬡

BREATHING EXERCISE: [   ]

PRAYER \ MEDITATION \ READING NOTES

NOTES / APPOINTMENTS FOR THE DAY:

Now Plan Your Day ☺

Date: _____

TO DO BY PRIORITY

- ○
- ○
- ○
- ○
- ○
- ○
- ○
- ○
- ○
- ○

Date: _____

TO DO BY PRIORITY

- ○
- ○
- ○
- ○
- ○
- ○
- ○
- ○
- ○
- ○

Date: _____

TO DO BY PRIORITY

- ○
- ○
- ○
- ○
- ○
- ○
- ○
- ○
- ○
- ○

Date: _____

TO DO BY PRIORITY

- ○
- ○
- ○
- ○
- ○
- ○
- ○
- ○
- ○
- ○

Date: _____

TO DO BY PRIORITY

- ○ _____
- ○ _____
- ○ _____
- ○ _____
- ○ _____
- ○ _____
- ○ _____
- ○ _____
- ○ _____
- ○ _____

Date: _____

TO DO BY PRIORITY

- ○ _____
- ○ _____
- ○ _____
- ○ _____
- ○ _____
- ○ _____
- ○ _____
- ○ _____
- ○ _____
- ○ _____

Date: _____

TO DO BY PRIORITY

- ○ _____
- ○ _____
- ○ _____
- ○ _____
- ○ _____
- ○ _____
- ○ _____
- ○ _____
- ○ _____
- ○ _____

Date: _____

TO DO BY PRIORITY

- ○ _____
- ○ _____
- ○ _____
- ○ _____
- ○ _____
- ○ _____
- ○ _____
- ○ _____
- ○ _____
- ○ _____

NOTES

"Be very careful how you live, not as unwise but as wise, making the most of every opportunity"
- Ephesians 5:15-16

Weekly Goal Strategies

Goal Area: ....

_____
_____
_____
_____
_____
_____
_____
_____
_____
_____
_____
_____
_____

Goal Area: ....

_____
_____
_____
_____
_____
_____
_____
_____
_____
_____
_____

Goal Area: ....

_____
_____
_____
_____
_____
_____
_____
_____
_____
_____
_____
_____

Goal Area: ....

_____
_____
_____
_____
_____
_____
_____
_____
_____
_____
_____
_____

Weekly Goal Strategies

Goal Area: ....

_____
_____
_____
_____
_____
_____
_____
_____
_____
_____
_____
_____
_____

Goal Area: ....

_____
_____
_____
_____
_____
_____
_____
_____
_____
_____
_____

Goal Area: ....

_____
_____
_____
_____
_____
_____
_____
_____
_____
_____
_____
_____

Goal Area: ....

_____
_____
_____
_____
_____
_____
_____
_____
_____
_____
_____
_____
_____
_____

Sunday

Trust in the LORD with all your heart and lean not on your own understanding; in all your ways submit to him, and he will make your paths straight.
——Proverbs 3:5–6

MORNING ROUTINE

DECREES / AFFIRMATION:

THINGS I AM THANKFUL TO GOD FOR TODAY:

1.
2.
3.

TYPE OF EXERCISE

AMOUNT (DISTANCE, TIME, SETS, REPS, WEIGHT)

CUPS OF WATER: ◇◇◇◇◇◇◇◇   BREATHING EXERCISE: ☐

PRAYER \ MEDITATION \ READING NOTES

NOTES / APPOINTMENTS FOR THE DAY:

Now Plan Your Day ☺

Monday

We want each of you to show this same diligence to the very end, so that what you hope for may be fully realized.
—Hebrews 6:11

MORNING ROUTINE

DECREES / AFFIRMATION:

THINGS I AM THANKFUL TO GOD FOR TODAY:

1. _____
2. _____
3. _____

TYPE OF EXERCISE

AMOUNT (DISTANCE, TIME, SETS, REPS, WEIGHT)

_____

_____

CUPS OF WATER: ◊◊◊◊◊◊◊◊   BREATHING EXERCISE: [   ]

PRAYER \ MEDITATION \ READING NOTES

NOTES / APPOINTMENTS FOR THE DAY:

Now Plan Your Day ☺

Tuesday

Take delight in the LORD, and he will give you the desires of your heart.
——Psalm 37:4

MORNING ROUTINE

DECREES / AFFIRMATION:

THINGS I AM THANKFUL TO GOD FOR TODAY:

1. _____
2. _____
3. _____

TYPE OF EXERCISE

AMOUNT (DISTANCE, TIME, SETS, REPS, WEIGHT)

CUPS OF WATER: ⬭⬭⬭⬭⬭⬭⬭⬭   BREATHING EXERCISE: [_____]

PRAYER \ MEDITATION \ READING NOTES

NOTES / APPOINTMENTS FOR THE DAY:

Now Plan Your Day ☺

Wednesday

But blessed is the one who trusts in the LORD, whose confidence is in him.
——Jeremiah 17:7

MORNING ROUTINE

DECREES / AFFIRMATION:

THINGS I AM THANKFUL TO GOD FOR TODAY:

1.
2.
3.

TYPE OF EXERCISE

AMOUNT (DISTANCE, TIME, SETS, REPS, WEIGHT)

CUPS OF WATER: 〇〇〇〇〇〇〇〇

BREATHING EXERCISE:

PRAYER \ MEDITATION \ READING NOTES

NOTES / APPOINTMENTS FOR THE DAY:

Now Plan Your Day

39

Thursday

Be anxious for nothing, but in everything by prayer and supplication, with thanksgiving, let your requests be made known to God; and the peace of God, which surpasses all understanding, will guard your hearts and minds through Christ Jesus.
——Philippians 4:6–7

MORNING ROUTINE

DECREES / AFFIRMATION:

THINGS I AM THANKFUL TO GOD FOR TODAY:

1. ....
2. ....
3. ....

TYPE OF EXERCISE

AMOUNT (DISTANCE, TIME, SETS, REPS, WEIGHT)

CUPS OF WATER: ⬡⬡⬡⬡⬡⬡⬡⬡   BREATHING EXERCISE: ☐

PRAYER \ MEDITATION \ READING NOTES

NOTES / APPOINTMENTS FOR THE DAY:

Now Plan Your Day ☺

Friday

I keep my eyes always on the Lord. With him at my right hand, I will not be shaken.
——Psalm 16:8

MORNING ROUTINE

DECREES / AFFIRMATION:

THINGS I AM THANKFUL TO GOD FOR TODAY:

1. _____
2. _____
3. _____

TYPE OF EXERCISE

AMOUNT (DISTANCE, TIME, SETS, REPS, WEIGHT)

CUPS OF WATER: ⬭⬭⬭⬭⬭⬭⬭

BREATHING EXERCISE: ☐

PRAYER \ MEDITATION \ READING NOTES

NOTES / APPOINTMENTS FOR THE DAY:

Now Plan Your Day :)

Saturday

And whatever you do, do it heartily, as to the Lord and not to men.
—Colossians 3:23

MORNING ROUTINE

DECREES / AFFIRMATION:

THINGS I AM THANKFUL TO GOD FOR TODAY:

1. ....
2. ....
3. ....

TYPE OF EXERCISE

AMOUNT (DISTANCE, TIME, SETS, REPS, WEIGHT)

CUPS OF WATER: ⬭⬭⬭⬭⬭⬭⬭

BREATHING EXERCISE: [   ]

PRAYER \ MEDITATION \ READING NOTES

NOTES / APPOINTMENTS FOR THE DAY:

Now Plan Your Day

Date: _____

TO DO BY PRIORITY
○ _____
○ _____
○ _____
○ _____
○ _____
○ _____
○ _____
○ _____
○ _____
○ _____

Date: _____

TO DO BY PRIORITY
○ _____
○ _____
○ _____
○ _____
○ _____
○ _____
○ _____
○ _____
○ _____
○ _____

Date: _____

TO DO BY PRIORITY
○ _____
○ _____
○ _____
○ _____
○ _____
○ _____
○ _____
○ _____
○ _____
○ _____

Date: _____

TO DO BY PRIORITY
○ _____
○ _____
○ _____
○ _____
○ _____
○ _____
○ _____
○ _____
○ _____
○ _____

Date: ....

TO DO BY PRIORITY

○ _____
○ _____
○ _____
○ _____
○ _____
○ _____
○ _____
○ _____
○ _____
○ _____

Date: ....

TO DO BY PRIORITY

○ _____
○ _____
○ _____
○ _____
○ _____
○ _____
○ _____
○ _____
○ _____
○ _____

Date: ....

TO DO BY PRIORITY

○ _____
○ _____
○ _____
○ _____
○ _____
○ _____
○ _____
○ _____
○ _____
○ _____

Date: ....

TO DO BY PRIORITY

○ _____
○ _____
○ _____
○ _____
○ _____
○ _____
○ _____
○ _____
○ _____
○ _____

NOTES

Be very careful how you live, not as unwise but as wise, making the most of every opportunity.
—Ephesians 5:15–16

Weekly Goal Strategies

Goal Area: ....

_____
_____
_____
_____
_____
_____
_____
_____
_____
_____
_____
_____

Goal Area: ....

_____
_____
_____
_____
_____
_____
_____
_____
_____
_____
_____

Goal Area: ....

_____
_____
_____
_____
_____
_____
_____
_____
_____
_____
_____

Goal Area: ....

_____
_____
_____
_____
_____
_____
_____
_____
_____
_____
_____
_____

Weekly Goal Strategies

Goal Area:

Goal Area:

Goal Area:

Goal Area:

Sunday

Jesus looked at them and said, "With man this is impossible, but with God all things are possible."
—Matthew 19:26

MORNING ROUTINE

DECREES / AFFIRMATION:

THINGS I AM THANKFUL TO GOD FOR TODAY:

1.
2.
3.

TYPE OF EXERCISE

AMOUNT (DISTANCE, TIME, SETS, REPS, WEIGHT)

CUPS OF WATER: 〇〇〇〇〇〇〇〇   BREATHING EXERCISE:

PRAYER \ MEDITATION \ READING NOTES

NOTES / APPOINTMENTS FOR THE DAY:

Now Plan Your Day

Monday

For I, the Lord your God, will hold your right hand, Saying to you,
"Fear not, I will help you."
—Isaiah 41:13

MORNING ROUTINE

DECREES / AFFIRMATION:

THINGS I AM THANKFUL TO GOD FOR TODAY:

1.
2.
3.

TYPE OF EXERCISE

AMOUNT (DISTANCE, TIME, SETS, REPS, WEIGHT)

CUPS OF WATER: ⬡⬡⬡⬡⬡⬡⬡   BREATHING EXERCISE: ▭

PRAYER \ MEDITATION \ READING NOTES

NOTES / APPOINTMENTS FOR THE DAY:

Now Plan Your Day

Tuesday

For God has not given us a spirit of fear and timidity, but of power, love, and self-discipline.
—2 Timothy 1:7

MORNING ROUTINE

DECREES / AFFIRMATION:

THINGS I AM THANKFUL TO GOD FOR TODAY:

1.
2.
3.

TYPE OF EXERCISE

AMOUNT (DISTANCE, TIME, SETS, REPS, WEIGHT)

CUPS OF WATER: ⬡⬡⬡⬡⬡⬡⬡⬡   BREATHING EXERCISE: [   ]

PRAYER \ MEDITATION \ READING NOTES

NOTES / APPOINTMENTS FOR THE DAY:

Now Plan Your Day ☺

Wednesday

You will keep in perfect peace those whose minds are steadfast,
because they trust in you.
——Isaiah 26:3

MORNING ROUTINE

DECREES / AFFIRMATION:

THINGS I AM THANKFUL TO GOD FOR TODAY:

1.
2.
3.

TYPE OF EXERCISE

AMOUNT (DISTANCE, TIME, SETS, REPS, WEIGHT)

CUPS OF WATER: ⬭⬭⬭⬭⬭⬭⬭

BREATHING EXERCISE:

PRAYER \ MEDITATION \ READING NOTES

NOTES / APPOINTMENTS FOR THE DAY:

Now Plan Your Day ☺

Thursday

For I can do everything through Christ, who gives me strength.
——Philippians 4:13

MORNING ROUTINE

DECREES / AFFIRMATION:

THINGS I AM THANKFUL TO GOD FOR TODAY:

1.
2.
3.

TYPE OF EXERCISE

AMOUNT (DISTANCE, TIME, SETS, REPS, WEIGHT)

CUPS OF WATER: ⬡⬡⬡⬡⬡⬡⬡

BREATHING EXERCISE: [   ]

PRAYER \ MEDITATION \ READING NOTES

NOTES / APPOINTMENTS FOR THE DAY:

Now Plan Your Day ☺

Friday

"For I know the plans I have for you," declares the Lord, "plans to prosper you and not to harm you, plans to give you hope and a future."
——Jeremiah 29:11

MORNING ROUTINE

DECREES / AFFIRMATION:

THINGS I AM THANKFUL TO GOD FOR TODAY:

1. ....
2. ....
3. ....

TYPE OF EXERCISE

AMOUNT (DISTANCE, TIME, SETS, REPS, WEIGHT)

CUPS OF WATER: BREATHING EXERCISE:

PRAYER \ MEDITATION \ READING NOTES

NOTES / APPOINTMENTS FOR THE DAY:

Now Plan Your Day

Saturday

In the same way, faith by itself, if it is not accompanied by action, is dead.
——James 2:17

MORNING ROUTINE

DECREES / AFFIRMATION:

THINGS I AM THANKFUL TO GOD FOR TODAY:

1.
2.
3.

TYPE OF EXERCISE

AMOUNT (DISTANCE, TIME, SETS, REPS, WEIGHT)

CUPS OF WATER: 🌢🌢🌢🌢🌢🌢🌢   BREATHING EXERCISE: ☐

PRAYER \ MEDITATION \ READING NOTES

NOTES / APPOINTMENTS FOR THE DAY:

Now Plan Your Day ☺

Date: _____

TO DO BY PRIORITY
○ _____
○ _____
○ _____
○ _____
○ _____
○ _____
○ _____
○ _____
○ _____
○ _____

Date: _____

TO DO BY PRIORITY
○ _____
○ _____
○ _____
○ _____
○ _____
○ _____
○ _____
○ _____
○ _____
○ _____

Date: _____

TO DO BY PRIORITY
○ _____
○ _____
○ _____
○ _____
○ _____
○ _____
○ _____
○ _____
○ _____
○ _____

Date: _____

TO DO BY PRIORITY
○ _____
○ _____
○ _____
○ _____
○ _____
○ _____
○ _____
○ _____
○ _____
○ _____

Date: _____

○ _____
○ _____
○ _____
○ _____
○ _____
○ _____
○ _____
○ _____
○ _____
○ _____

Date: _____

TO DO BY PRIORITY

○ _____
○ _____
○ _____
○ _____
○ _____
○ _____
○ _____
○ _____
○ _____
○ _____

Date: _____

TO DO BY PRIORITY

○ _____
○ _____
○ _____
○ _____
○ _____
○ _____
○ _____
○ _____
○ _____
○ _____

Date: _____

TO DO BY PRIORITY

○ _____
○ _____
○ _____
○ _____
○ _____
○ _____
○ _____
○ _____
○ _____
○ _____

NOTES

"Be very careful how you live, not as unwise but as wise, making the most of every opportunity"
- Ephesians 5:15-16

Weekly Goal Strategies

Goal Area: ....

_____
_____
_____
_____
_____
_____
_____
_____
_____
_____
_____

Goal Area: ....

_____
_____
_____
_____
_____
_____
_____
_____
_____
_____
_____

Goal Area: ....

_____
_____
_____
_____
_____
_____
_____
_____
_____
_____
_____

Goal Area: ....

_____
_____
_____
_____
_____
_____
_____
_____
_____
_____
_____

Weekly Goal Strategies

Goal Area:

Goal Area:

Goal Area:

Goal Area:

Sunday

Be very careful, then, how you live——not as unwise but as wise.
——Ephesians 5:15

MORNING ROUTINE

DECREES / AFFIRMATION:

THINGS I AM THANKFUL TO GOD FOR TODAY:

1.
2.
3.

TYPE OF EXERCISE

AMOUNT (DISTANCE, TIME, SETS, REPS, WEIGHT)

CUPS OF WATER: 🌢🌢🌢🌢🌢🌢🌢🌢

BREATHING EXERCISE:

PRAYER \ MEDITATION \ READING NOTES

NOTES / APPOINTMENTS FOR THE DAY:

Now Plan Your Day ☺

Monday

For I, the Lord your God, will hold your right hand, Saying to you,
"Fear not, I will help you."
—Isaiah 41:13

MORNING ROUTINE

DECREES / AFFIRMATION:

THINGS I AM THANKFUL TO GOD FOR TODAY:

1.
2.
3.

TYPE OF EXERCISE

AMOUNT (DISTANCE, TIME, SETS, REPS, WEIGHT)

CUPS OF WATER:

BREATHING EXERCISE:

PRAYER \ MEDITATION \ READING NOTES

NOTES / APPOINTMENTS FOR THE DAY:

Now Plan Your Day

Tuesday

I instruct you in the way of wisdom and lead you along straight paths.
——Proverbs 4:11

MORNING ROUTINE

DECREES / AFFIRMATION:

THINGS I AM THANKFUL TO GOD FOR TODAY:

1. ....
2. ....
3. ....

TYPE OF EXERCISE

AMOUNT (DISTANCE, TIME, SETS, REPS, WEIGHT)

CUPS OF WATER: ⬦⬦⬦⬦⬦⬦⬦⬦   BREATHING EXERCISE: [   ]

PRAYER \ MEDITATION \ READING NOTES

NOTES / APPOINTMENTS FOR THE DAY:

Now Plan Your Day ☺

Wednesday

But seek first his kingdom and his righteousness, and all these things will be
given to you as well.
—Matthew 6:33

MORNING ROUTINE

DECREES / AFFIRMATION:

THINGS I AM THANKFUL TO GOD FOR TODAY:

1.
2.
3.

TYPE OF EXERCISE

AMOUNT (DISTANCE, TIME, SETS, REPS, WEIGHT)

CUPS OF WATER:

BREATHING EXERCISE:

PRAYER \ MEDITATION \ READING NOTES

NOTES / APPOINTMENTS FOR THE DAY:

Now Plan Your Day ☺

Thursday

In everything he did he had great success, because the LORD was with him.
—1 Samuel 18:14

MORNING ROUTINE

DECREES / AFFIRMATION:

THINGS I AM THANKFUL TO GOD FOR TODAY:

1.
2.
3.

TYPE OF EXERCISE

AMOUNT (DISTANCE, TIME, SETS, REPS, WEIGHT)

CUPS OF WATER: ⬦⬦⬦⬦⬦⬦⬦⬦

BREATHING EXERCISE:

PRAYER \ MEDITATION \ READING NOTES

NOTES / APPOINTMENTS FOR THE DAY:

Now Plan Your Day ☺

Friday

Study this Book of Instruction continually. Meditate on it day and night so you will be sure to obey everything written in it. Only then will you prosper and succeed in all you do.
——Joshua 1:8

MORNING ROUTINE

DECREES / AFFIRMATION:

THINGS I AM THANKFUL TO GOD FOR TODAY:

1.
2.
3.

TYPE OF EXERCISE

AMOUNT (DISTANCE, TIME, SETS, REPS, WEIGHT)

CUPS OF WATER: ⬭⬭⬭⬭⬭⬭⬭   BREATHING EXERCISE:

PRAYER \ MEDITATION \ READING NOTES

NOTES / APPOINTMENTS FOR THE DAY:

Now Plan Your Day ☺

Saturday

And we know that in all things God works for the good of those who love him,
who have been called according to his purpose.
—Romans 8:28

MORNING ROUTINE

DECREES / AFFIRMATION:

THINGS I AM THANKFUL TO GOD FOR TODAY:

1.
2.
3.

TYPE OF EXERCISE

AMOUNT (DISTANCE, TIME, SETS, REPS, WEIGHT)

CUPS OF WATER: ⬭⬭⬭⬭⬭⬭⬭⬭

BREATHING EXERCISE:

PRAYER \ MEDITATION \ READING NOTES

NOTES / APPOINTMENTS FOR THE DAY:

Now Plan Your Day ☺

Date: _____

○ _____
○ _____
○ _____
○ _____
○ _____
○ _____
○ _____
○ _____
○ _____
○ _____

Date: _____

TO DO BY PRIORITY

○ _____
○ _____
○ _____
○ _____
○ _____
○ _____
○ _____
○ _____
○ _____
○ _____

Date: _____

TO DO BY PRIORITY

○ _____
○ _____
○ _____
○ _____
○ _____
○ _____
○ _____
○ _____
○ _____
○ _____

Date: _____

TO DO BY PRIORITY

○ _____
○ _____
○ _____
○ _____
○ _____
○ _____
○ _____
○ _____
○ _____
○ _____

Date: _____

TO DO BY PRIORITY

- ○ _____
- ○ _____
- ○ _____
- ○ _____
- ○ _____
- ○ _____
- ○ _____
- ○ _____
- ○ _____
- ○ _____

Date: _____

TO DO BY PRIORITY

- ○ _____
- ○ _____
- ○ _____
- ○ _____
- ○ _____
- ○ _____
- ○ _____
- ○ _____
- ○ _____
- ○ _____

Date: _____

TO DO BY PRIORITY

- ○ _____
- ○ _____
- ○ _____
- ○ _____
- ○ _____
- ○ _____
- ○ _____
- ○ _____
- ○ _____
- ○ _____

Date: _____

TO DO BY PRIORITY

- ○ _____
- ○ _____
- ○ _____
- ○ _____
- ○ _____
- ○ _____
- ○ _____
- ○ _____
- ○ _____
- ○ _____

NOTES

"Be very careful how you live, not as unwise but as wise, making the most of every opportunity"
- Ephesians 5:15-16

Month:

SUNDAY	MONDAY	TUESDAY	WEDNESDAY

THURSDAY	FRIDAY	SATURDAY	NOTES

Weekly Goal Strategies

Goal Area:

Goal Area:

Goal Area:

Goal Area:

Weekly Goal Strategies

Goal Area:

Goal Area:

Goal Area:

Goal Area:

Sunday

See, I am doing a new thing! Now it springs up; do you not perceive it?
I am making a way in the wilderness and streams in the wasteland.
----Isaiah 43:19

MORNING ROUTINE

DECREES / AFFIRMATION:

THINGS I AM THANKFUL TO GOD FOR TODAY:

1.
2.
3.

TYPE OF EXERCISE

AMOUNT (DISTANCE, TIME, SETS, REPS, WEIGHT)

CUPS OF WATER: ○○○○○○○○   BREATHING EXERCISE: [　　　]

PRAYER \ MEDITATION \ READING NOTES

NOTES / APPOINTMENTS FOR THE DAY:

Now Plan Your Day ☺

Monday

Therefore, if anyone is in Christ, the new creation has come:
The old has gone, the new is here!
—2 Corinthians 5:17

MORNING ROUTINE

DECREES / AFFIRMATION:

THINGS I AM THANKFUL TO GOD FOR TODAY:

1. ....
2. ....
3. ....

TYPE OF EXERCISE

AMOUNT (DISTANCE, TIME, SETS, REPS, WEIGHT)

CUPS OF WATER: ⬭⬭⬭⬭⬭⬭⬭⬭   BREATHING EXERCISE: [   ]

PRAYER \ MEDITATION \ READING NOTES

NOTES / APPOINTMENTS FOR THE DAY:

Now Plan Your Day

Tuesday

Since you are my rock and my fortress, for the sake of your name lead and guide me.
——Psalm 31:3

MORNING ROUTINE

DECREES / AFFIRMATION:

THINGS I AM THANKFUL TO GOD FOR TODAY:

1.
2.
3.

TYPE OF EXERCISE

AMOUNT (DISTANCE, TIME, SETS, REPS, WEIGHT)

CUPS OF WATER: ◊◊◊◊◊◊◊◊   BREATHING EXERCISE: [   ]

PRAYER \ MEDITATION \ READING NOTES

NOTES / APPOINTMENTS FOR THE DAY:

Now Plan Your Day ☺

Wednesday

Show me your ways, Lord, teach me your paths.
——Psalm 25:4

MORNING ROUTINE

DECREES / AFFIRMATION:

THINGS I AM THANKFUL TO GOD FOR TODAY:

1. _____
2. _____
3. _____

TYPE OF EXERCISE

AMOUNT (DISTANCE, TIME, SETS, REPS, WEIGHT)

CUPS OF WATER: ⬡⬡⬡⬡⬡⬡⬡   BREATHING EXERCISE: [ ]

PRAYER \ MEDITATION \ READING NOTES

NOTES / APPOINTMENTS FOR THE DAY:

Now Plan Your Day

Thursday

There is a time for everything, and a season for every activity under the heavens.
—Ecclesiastes 3:1

DECREES / AFFIRMATION:

THINGS I AM THANKFUL TO GOD FOR TODAY:

1.
2.
3.

TYPE OF EXERCISE

AMOUNT (DISTANCE, TIME, SETS, REPS, WEIGHT)

CUPS OF WATER: ⬦⬦⬦⬦⬦⬦⬦

BREATHING EXERCISE: ☐

PRAYER \ MEDITATION \ READING NOTES

NOTES / APPOINTMENTS FOR THE DAY:

Now Plan Your Day ☺

Friday

For I command you today to love the Lord your God, to walk in obedience to him, and to keep his commands, decrees and laws; then you will live and increase, and the Lord your God will bless you in the land you are entering to possess.
——Deuteronomy 30:16

MORNING ROUTINE

DECREES / AFFIRMATION:

THINGS I AM THANKFUL TO GOD FOR TODAY:

1. ....
2. ....
3. ....

TYPE OF EXERCISE

AMOUNT (DISTANCE, TIME, SETS, REPS, WEIGHT)

CUPS OF WATER: ⬦⬦⬦⬦⬦⬦⬦⬦   BREATHING EXERCISE: ▢

PRAYER \ MEDITATION \ READING NOTES

NOTES / APPOINTMENTS FOR THE DAY:

Now Plan Your Day ☺

Saturday

When Jesus spoke again to the people, he said, "I am the light of the world. Whoever follows me will never walk in darkness, but will have the light of life."
—John 8:12

MORNING ROUTINE

DECREES / AFFIRMATION:

THINGS I AM THANKFUL TO GOD FOR TODAY:

1.
2.
3.

TYPE OF EXERCISE

AMOUNT (DISTANCE, TIME, SETS, REPS, WEIGHT)

CUPS OF WATER: 🜄🜄🜄🜄🜄🜄🜄   BREATHING EXERCISE: [＿＿＿]

PRAYER \ MEDITATION \ READING NOTES

NOTES / APPOINTMENTS FOR THE DAY:

Now Plan Your Day ☺

Date: ....

TO DO BY PRIORITY

○ _____
○ _____
○ _____
○ _____
○ _____
○ _____
○ _____
○ _____
○ _____
○ _____

Date: ....

TO DO BY PRIORITY

○ _____
○ _____
○ _____
○ _____
○ _____
○ _____
○ _____
○ _____
○ _____
○ _____

Date: ....

TO DO BY PRIORITY

○ _____
○ _____
○ _____
○ _____
○ _____
○ _____
○ _____
○ _____
○ _____
○ _____

Date: ....

TO DO BY PRIORITY

○ _____
○ _____
○ _____
○ _____
○ _____
○ _____
○ _____
○ _____
○ _____
○ _____

Date: _____

TO DO BY PRIORITY

○ _____
○ _____
○ _____
○ _____
○ _____
○ _____
○ _____
○ _____
○ _____
○ _____

Date: _____

TO DO BY PRIORITY

○ _____
○ _____
○ _____
○ _____
○ _____
○ _____
○ _____
○ _____
○ _____
○ _____

Date: _____

TO DO BY PRIORITY

○ _____
○ _____
○ _____
○ _____
○ _____
○ _____
○ _____
○ _____
○ _____
○ _____

Date: _____

TO DO BY PRIORITY

○ _____
○ _____
○ _____
○ _____
○ _____
○ _____
○ _____
○ _____
○ _____
○ _____

NOTES

"Be very careful how you live, not as unwise but as wise, making the most of every opportunity"
- Ephesians 5:15-16

Weekly Goal Strategies

Goal Area:

_____

Goal Area:

_____

Goal Area:

_____

Goal Area:

_____

Weekly Goal Strategies

Goal Area:

Goal Area:

Goal Area:

Goal Area:

Sunday

Give careful thought to the paths for your feet and be steadfast in all your ways. Do not turn to the right or the left; keep your foot from evil.
—Proverbs 4:26–27

MORNING ROUTINE

DECREES / AFFIRMATION:

THINGS I AM THANKFUL TO GOD FOR TODAY:

1.
2.
3.

TYPE OF EXERCISE

AMOUNT (DISTANCE, TIME, SETS, REPS, WEIGHT)

CUPS OF WATER: 〇〇〇〇〇〇〇〇

BREATHING EXERCISE:

PRAYER \ MEDITATION \ READING NOTES

NOTES / APPOINTMENTS FOR THE DAY:

Now Plan Your Day

Monday

Surely God is my help; the Lord is the one who sustains me.
——Psalm 54:4

MORNING ROUTINE

DECREES / AFFIRMATION:

THINGS I AM THANKFUL TO GOD FOR TODAY:

1.
2.
3.

TYPE OF EXERCISE

AMOUNT (DISTANCE, TIME, SETS, REPS, WEIGHT)

CUPS OF WATER: ⬦⬦⬦⬦⬦⬦⬦ BREATHING EXERCISE: ☐

PRAYER \ MEDITATION \ READING NOTES

NOTES / APPOINTMENTS FOR THE DAY:

Now Plan Your Day ☺

Tuesday

I pray that the eyes of your heart may be enlightened in order that you may know the hope to which he has called you, the riches of his glorious inheritance in his holy people.
—Ephesians 1:18

MORNING ROUTINE

DECREES / AFFIRMATION:

THINGS I AM THANKFUL TO GOD FOR TODAY:

1.
2.
3.

TYPE OF EXERCISE

AMOUNT (DISTANCE, TIME, SETS, REPS, WEIGHT)

CUPS OF WATER: ⬤⬤⬤⬤⬤⬤⬤⬤

BREATHING EXERCISE:

PRAYER \ MEDITATION \ READING NOTES

NOTES / APPOINTMENTS FOR THE DAY:

Now Plan Your Day ☺

Wednesday

But thanks be to God! He gives us the victory through our Lord Jesus Christ.
—1 Corinthians 15:57

MORNING ROUTINE

DECREES / AFFIRMATION:

THINGS I AM THANKFUL TO GOD FOR TODAY:

1.
2.
3.

TYPE OF EXERCISE

AMOUNT (DISTANCE, TIME, SETS, REPS, WEIGHT)

CUPS OF WATER: ⬡⬡⬡⬡⬡⬡⬡ BREATHING EXERCISE: ⬜

PRAYER \ MEDITATION \ READING NOTES

NOTES / APPOINTMENTS FOR THE DAY:

 **Now Plan Your Day** ☺

Thursday

I have come that they may have life, and that they may have it more abundantly.
—John 10:10

MORNING ROUTINE

DECREES / AFFIRMATION:

THINGS I AM THANKFUL TO GOD FOR TODAY:

1. _____
2. _____
3. _____

TYPE OF EXERCISE

AMOUNT (DISTANCE, TIME, SETS, REPS, WEIGHT)

CUPS OF WATER: ⬢⬢⬢⬢⬢⬢⬢⬢   BREATHING EXERCISE: [   ]

PRAYER \ MEDITATION \ READING NOTES

NOTES / APPOINTMENTS FOR THE DAY:

Now Plan Your Day ☺

Friday

Therefore we do not lose heart. Though outwardly we are wasting away,
yet inwardly we are being renewed day by day.
—2 Corinthians 4:16–17

MORNING ROUTINE

DECREES / AFFIRMATION:

THINGS I AM THANKFUL TO GOD FOR TODAY:

1.
2.
3.

TYPE OF EXERCISE

AMOUNT (DISTANCE, TIME, SETS, REPS, WEIGHT)

CUPS OF WATER: ⬡⬡⬡⬡⬡⬡⬡⬡

BREATHING EXERCISE:

PRAYER \ MEDITATION \ READING NOTES

NOTES / APPOINTMENTS FOR THE DAY:

Now Plan Your Day ☺

Saturday

For the Lord gives wisdom, from his mouth come knowledge and understanding.
——Proverbs 2:6

MORNING ROUTINE

DECREES / AFFIRMATION:

THINGS I AM THANKFUL TO GOD FOR TODAY:

1.
2.
3.

TYPE OF EXERCISE

AMOUNT (DISTANCE, TIME, SETS, REPS, WEIGHT)

CUPS OF WATER: ○○○○○○○○   BREATHING EXERCISE:

PRAYER \ MEDITATION \ READING NOTES

NOTES / APPOINTMENTS FOR THE DAY:

Now Plan Your Day

Date: _____

TO DO BY PRIORITY

○ _____
○ _____
○ _____
○ _____
○ _____
○ _____
○ _____
○ _____
○ _____
○ _____

Date: _____

TO DO BY PRIORITY

○ _____
○ _____
○ _____
○ _____
○ _____
○ _____
○ _____
○ _____
○ _____
○ _____

Date: _____

TO DO BY PRIORITY

○ _____
○ _____
○ _____
○ _____
○ _____
○ _____
○ _____
○ _____
○ _____
○ _____

Date: _____

TO DO BY PRIORITY

○ _____
○ _____
○ _____
○ _____
○ _____
○ _____
○ _____
○ _____
○ _____
○ _____

Date: ....

TO DO BY PRIORITY

○
○
○
○
○
○
○
○
○
○

Date: ....

TO DO BY PRIORITY

○
○
○
○
○
○
○
○
○
○

Date: ....

TO DO BY PRIORITY

○
○
○
○
○
○
○
○
○
○

Date: ....

TO DO BY PRIORITY

○
○
○
○
○
○
○
○
○
○

NOTES

"Be very careful how you live, not as unwise but as wise, making the most of every opportunity"
- Ephesians 5:15-16

Weekly Goal Strategies

Goal Area:

Goal Area:

Goal Area:

Goal Area:

Weekly Goal Strategies

Goal Area:

Goal Area:

Goal Area:

Goal Area:

Sunday

If any of you lacks wisdom, you should ask God, who gives generously to all without finding fault, and it will be given to you.
—James 1:5

MORNING ROUTINE

DECREES / AFFIRMATION:

THINGS I AM THANKFUL. TO GOD FOR TODAY:

1. _____
2. _____
3. _____

TYPE OF EXERCISE

AMOUNT (DISTANCE, TIME, SETS, REPS, WEIGHT)

CUPS OF WATER: ⬡⬡⬡⬡⬡⬡⬡⬡   BREATHING EXERCISE: [　　]

PRAYER \ MEDITATION \ READING NOTES

NOTES / APPOINTMENTS FOR THE DAY:

Now Plan Your Day ☺

Monday

The Lord himself goes before you and will be with you; he will never leave you nor forsake you. Do not be afraid; do not be discouraged.
—Deuteronomy 31:8

MORNING ROUTINE

DECREES / AFFIRMATION:

THINGS I AM THANKFUL TO GOD FOR TODAY:

1.
2.
3.

TYPE OF EXERCISE

AMOUNT (DISTANCE, TIME, SETS, REPS, WEIGHT)

CUPS OF WATER: ⬡⬡⬡⬡⬡⬡⬡   BREATHING EXERCISE: [   ]

PRAYER \ MEDITATION \ READING NOTES

NOTES / APPOINTMENTS FOR THE DAY:

Now Plan Your Day :)

Tuesday

The Lord says, "I will guide you along the best pathway for your life.
I will advise you and watch over you."
——Psalm 32:8

MORNING ROUTINE

DECREES / AFFIRMATION:

THINGS I AM THANKFUL TO GOD FOR TODAY:

1.
2.
3.

TYPE OF EXERCISE

AMOUNT (DISTANCE, TIME, SETS, REPS, WEIGHT)

CUPS OF WATER: ⬦⬦⬦⬦⬦⬦⬦⬦   BREATHING EXERCISE: ☐

PRAYER \ MEDITATION \ READING NOTES

NOTES / APPOINTMENTS FOR THE DAY:

Now Plan Your Day ☺

Wednesday

Therefore I tell you, whatever you ask for in prayer, believe that you have received it, and it will be yours.
—Mark 11:24

MORNING ROUTINE

DECREES / AFFIRMATION:

THINGS I AM THANKFUL TO GOD FOR TODAY:

1.
2.
3.

TYPE OF EXERCISE

AMOUNT (DISTANCE, TIME, SETS, REPS, WEIGHT)

CUPS OF WATER: ⬦⬦⬦⬦⬦⬦⬦   BREATHING EXERCISE: ☐

PRAYER \ MEDITATION \ READING NOTES

NOTES / APPOINTMENTS FOR THE DAY:

Now Plan Your Day ☺

Thursday

But those who hope in the LORD will renew their strength. They will soar on wings like eagles; they will run and not grow weary, they will walk and not be faint.
—Isaiah 40:31

MORNING ROUTINE

DECREES / AFFIRMATION:

THINGS I AM THANKFUL TO GOD FOR TODAY:

1.
2.
3.

TYPE OF EXERCISE

AMOUNT (DISTANCE, TIME, SETS, REPS, WEIGHT)

CUPS OF WATER: 〇〇〇〇〇〇〇〇   BREATHING EXERCISE: ☐

PRAYER \ MEDITATION \ READING NOTES

NOTES / APPOINTMENTS FOR THE DAY:

Now Plan Your Day ☺

Friday

Being confident of this, that he who began a good work in you will carry it on to completion until the day of Christ Jesus.
—Philippians 1:6

MORNING ROUTINE

DECREES / AFFIRMATION:

THINGS I AM THANKFUL TO GOD FOR TODAY:

1.
2.
3.

TYPE OF EXERCISE

AMOUNT (DISTANCE, TIME, SETS, REPS, WEIGHT)

CUPS OF WATER: ⬡⬡⬡⬡⬡⬡⬡   BREATHING EXERCISE: ☐

PRAYER \ MEDITATION \ READING NOTES

NOTES / APPOINTMENTS FOR THE DAY:

Now Plan Your Day 😊

Saturday

Consider it pure joy, my brothers and sisters, whenever you face trials of many kinds,
because you know that the testing of your faith produces perseverance.
——James 1:2–3

MORNING ROUTINE

DECREES / AFFIRMATION:

THINGS I AM THANKFUL TO GOD FOR TODAY:

1.
2.
3.

TYPE OF EXERCISE

AMOUNT (DISTANCE, TIME, SETS, REPS, WEIGHT)

CUPS OF WATER: ⬡⬡⬡⬡⬡⬡⬡⬡   BREATHING EXERCISE: ☐

PRAYER \ MEDITATION \ READING NOTES

NOTES / APPOINTMENTS FOR THE DAY:

Now Plan Your Day 😊

Date: _____

TO DO BY PRIORITY

- ○ _____
- ○ _____
- ○ _____
- ○ _____
- ○ _____
- ○ _____
- ○ _____
- ○ _____
- ○ _____
- ○ _____

Date: _____

TO DO BY PRIORITY

- ○ _____
- ○ _____
- ○ _____
- ○ _____
- ○ _____
- ○ _____
- ○ _____
- ○ _____
- ○ _____
- ○ _____

Date: _____

TO DO BY PRIORITY

- ○ _____
- ○ _____
- ○ _____
- ○ _____
- ○ _____
- ○ _____
- ○ _____
- ○ _____
- ○ _____
- ○ _____

Date: _____

TO DO BY PRIORITY

- ○ _____
- ○ _____
- ○ _____
- ○ _____
- ○ _____
- ○ _____
- ○ _____
- ○ _____
- ○ _____
- ○ _____

Date: _____

TO DO BY PRIORITY

- ○ _____
- ○ _____
- ○ _____
- ○ _____
- ○ _____
- ○ _____
- ○ _____
- ○ _____
- ○ _____
- ○ _____

Date: _____

TO DO BY PRIORITY

- ○ _____
- ○ _____
- ○ _____
- ○ _____
- ○ _____
- ○ _____
- ○ _____
- ○ _____
- ○ _____
- ○ _____

Date: _____

TO DO BY PRIORITY

- ○ _____
- ○ _____
- ○ _____
- ○ _____
- ○ _____
- ○ _____
- ○ _____
- ○ _____
- ○ _____
- ○ _____

Date: _____

TO DO BY PRIORITY

- ○ _____
- ○ _____
- ○ _____
- ○ _____
- ○ _____
- ○ _____
- ○ _____
- ○ _____
- ○ _____
- ○ _____

NOTES

"Be very careful how you live, not as unwise but as wise, making the most of every opportunity"
- Ephesians 5:15-16

Weekly Goal Strategies

Goal Area: _____

Goal Area: _____

Goal Area: _____

Goal Area: _____

Weekly Goal Strategies

Goal Area: _____

_____
_____
_____
_____
_____
_____
_____
_____
_____
_____
_____
_____
_____

Goal Area: _____

_____
_____
_____
_____
_____
_____
_____
_____
_____
_____
_____
_____
_____

Goal Area: _____

_____
_____
_____
_____
_____
_____
_____
_____
_____
_____
_____
_____
_____
_____

Goal Area: _____

_____
_____
_____
_____
_____
_____
_____
_____
_____
_____
_____
_____
_____
_____

Sunday

Cast your cares on the Lord and he will sustain you;
he will never let the righteous be shaken.
—Psalm 55:22

MORNING ROUTINE

DECREES / AFFIRMATION:

THINGS I AM THANKFUL TO GOD FOR TODAY:

1.
2.
3.

TYPE OF EXERCISE

AMOUNT (DISTANCE, TIME, SETS, REPS, WEIGHT)

CUPS OF WATER: ⬡⬡⬡⬡⬡⬡⬡⬡

BREATHING EXERCISE:

PRAYER \ MEDITATION \ READING NOTES

NOTES / APPOINTMENTS FOR THE DAY:

Now Plan Your Day ☺

Monday

Whether you turn to the right or to the left, your ears will hear a voice behind you, saying, "This is the way; walk in it."
—Isaiah 30:21

MORNING ROUTINE

DECREES / AFFIRMATION:

THINGS I AM THANKFUL TO GOD FOR TODAY:

1.
2.
3.

TYPE OF EXERCISE

AMOUNT (DISTANCE, TIME, SETS, REPS, WEIGHT)

CUPS OF WATER: ○○○○○○○○   BREATHING EXERCISE: ☐

PRAYER \ MEDITATION \ READING NOTES

NOTES / APPOINTMENTS FOR THE DAY:

Now Plan Your Day ☺

Tuesday

The Lord will guide you continually, giving you water when you are dry and restoring your strength. You will be like a well-watered garden, like an ever-flowing spring.
—Isaiah 58:11

MORNING ROUTINE

DECREES / AFFIRMATION:

THINGS I AM THANKFUL TO GOD FOR TODAY:

1.
2.
3.

TYPE OF EXERCISE

AMOUNT (DISTANCE, TIME, SETS, REPS, WEIGHT)

CUPS OF WATER: ⬤⬤⬤⬤⬤⬤⬤

BREATHING EXERCISE:

PRAYER \ MEDITATION \ READING NOTES

NOTES / APPOINTMENTS FOR THE DAY:

Now Plan Your Day ☺

Wednesday

May he give you the desire of your heart and make all your plans succeed.
—Psalm 20:4

MORNING ROUTINE

DECREES / AFFIRMATION:

THINGS I AM THANKFUL TO GOD FOR TODAY:

1.
2.
3.

TYPE OF EXERCISE

AMOUNT (DISTANCE, TIME, SETS, REPS, WEIGHT)

CUPS OF WATER: 〇〇〇〇〇〇〇〇

BREATHING EXERCISE: [   ]

PRAYER \ MEDITATION \ READING NOTES

NOTES / APPOINTMENTS FOR THE DAY:

Now Plan Your Day

113

Thursday

The plans of the diligent lead to profit as surely as haste leads to poverty.
-----Proverbs 21:5

MORNING ROUTINE

DECREES / AFFIRMATION:

THINGS I AM THANKFUL TO GOD FOR TODAY:

1.
2.
3.

TYPE OF EXERCISE

AMOUNT (DISTANCE, TIME, SETS, REPS, WEIGHT)

CUPS OF WATER:

BREATHING EXERCISE:

PRAYER \ MEDITATION \ READING NOTES

NOTES / APPOINTMENTS FOR THE DAY:

Now Plan Your Day ☺

Friday

Truly I tell you, if you have faith as small as a mustard seed, you can say to this mountain, "Move from here to there," and it will move. Nothing will be impossible for you.
—Matthew 17:20

MORNING ROUTINE

DECREES / AFFIRMATION:

THINGS I AM THANKFUL TO GOD FOR TODAY:

1.
2.
3.

TYPE OF EXERCISE

AMOUNT (DISTANCE, TIME, SETS, REPS, WEIGHT)

CUPS OF WATER: ⬡⬡⬡⬡⬡⬡⬡ BREATHING EXERCISE: ☐

PRAYER \ MEDITATION \ READING NOTES

NOTES / APPOINTMENTS FOR THE DAY:

Now Plan Your Day

115

Saturday

The soul of the sluggard craves and gets nothing,
while the soul of the diligent is richly supplied.
—Proverbs 13:4

MORNING ROUTINE

DECREES / AFFIRMATION:

THINGS I AM THANKFUL TO GOD FOR TODAY:

1.
2.
3.

TYPE OF EXERCISE

AMOUNT (DISTANCE, TIME, SETS, REPS, WEIGHT)

CUPS OF WATER: ⬡⬡⬡⬡⬡⬡⬡

BREATHING EXERCISE:

PRAYER \ MEDITATION \ READING NOTES

NOTES / APPOINTMENTS FOR THE DAY:

Now Plan Your Day ☺

Date: _____

TO DO BY PRIORITY

- ○ _____
- ○ _____
- ○ _____
- ○ _____
- ○ _____
- ○ _____
- ○ _____
- ○ _____
- ○ _____
- ○ _____

Date: _____

TO DO BY PRIORITY

- ○ _____
- ○ _____
- ○ _____
- ○ _____
- ○ _____
- ○ _____
- ○ _____
- ○ _____
- ○ _____
- ○ _____

Date: _____

TO DO BY PRIORITY

- ○ _____
- ○ _____
- ○ _____
- ○ _____
- ○ _____
- ○ _____
- ○ _____
- ○ _____
- ○ _____
- ○ _____

Date: _____

TO DO BY PRIORITY

- ○ _____
- ○ _____
- ○ _____
- ○ _____
- ○ _____
- ○ _____
- ○ _____
- ○ _____
- ○ _____
- ○ _____

Date: ....

TO DO BY PRIORITY

○ _____
○ _____
○ _____
○ _____
○ _____
○ _____
○ _____
○ _____
○ _____
○ _____

Date: ....

TO DO BY PRIORITY

○ _____
○ _____
○ _____
○ _____
○ _____
○ _____
○ _____
○ _____
○ _____
○ _____

Date: ....

TO DO BY PRIORITY

○ _____
○ _____
○ _____
○ _____
○ _____
○ _____
○ _____
○ _____
○ _____
○ _____

Date: ....

TO DO BY PRIORITY

○ _____
○ _____
○ _____
○ _____
○ _____
○ _____
○ _____
○ _____
○ _____
○ _____

NOTES

"Be very careful how you live, not as unwise but as wise, making the most of every opportunity"
- Ephesians 5:15-16

Weekly Goal Strategies

Goal Area: ....

Goal Area: ....

Goal Area: ....

Goal Area: ....

Weekly Goal Strategies

Goal Area:

Goal Area:

Goal Area:

Goal Area:

Sunday

*And let us not grow weary of doing good, for in due season we will reap,
if we do not give up.*
—Galatians 6:9

MORNING ROUTINE

DECREES / AFFIRMATION:

THINGS I AM THANKFUL TO GOD FOR TODAY:

1. ....
2. ....
3. ....

TYPE OF EXERCISE

AMOUNT (DISTANCE, TIME, SETS, REPS, WEIGHT)

CUPS OF WATER: 　　　　　　　

BREATHING EXERCISE: [＿＿＿]

PRAYER \ MEDITATION \ READING NOTES

NOTES / APPOINTMENTS FOR THE DAY:

Now Plan Your Day

Monday

In all toil there is profit, but mere talk leads only to poverty.
—Proverbs 14:23

MORNING ROUTINE

DECREES / AFFIRMATION:

THINGS I AM THANKFUL TO GOD FOR TODAY:

1. ....
2. ....
3. ....

TYPE OF EXERCISE

AMOUNT (DISTANCE, TIME, SETS, REPS, WEIGHT)

CUPS OF WATER: ⬦⬦⬦⬦⬦⬦⬦

BREATHING EXERCISE: ☐

PRAYER \ MEDITATION \ READING NOTES

NOTES / APPOINTMENTS FOR THE DAY:

Now Plan Your Day

Tuesday

I rejoice in your word like one who discovers a great treasure.
——Psalm 119:162

MORNING ROUTINE

DECREES / AFFIRMATION:

THINGS I AM THANKFUL TO GOD FOR TODAY:

1. ....
2. ....
3. ....

TYPE OF EXERCISE

AMOUNT (DISTANCE, TIME, SETS, REPS, WEIGHT)

CUPS OF WATER: ◊◊◊◊◊◊◊◊

BREATHING EXERCISE: [   ]

PRAYER \ MEDITATION \ READING NOTES

NOTES / APPOINTMENTS FOR THE DAY:

Now Plan Your Day

Wednesday

Wise words bring many benefits and hard work brings rewards.
—Proverbs 12:14

MORNING ROUTINE

DECREES / AFFIRMATION:

THINGS I AM THANKFUL TO GOD FOR TODAY:

1.
2.
3.

TYPE OF EXERCISE

AMOUNT (DISTANCE, TIME, SETS, REPS, WEIGHT)

CUPS OF WATER: ⬡⬡⬡⬡⬡⬡⬡⬡

BREATHING EXERCISE:

PRAYER \ MEDITATION \ READING NOTES

NOTES / APPOINTMENTS FOR THE DAY:

Now Plan Your Day ☺

Thursday

For everyone born of God overcomes the world. This is the victory that
has overcome the world, even our faith.
—1 John 5:4

MORNING ROUTINE

DECREES / AFFIRMATION:

THINGS I AM THANKFUL TO GOD FOR TODAY:

1.
2.
3.

TYPE OF EXERCISE

AMOUNT (DISTANCE, TIME, SETS, REPS, WEIGHT)

CUPS OF WATER: ⬡⬡⬡⬡⬡⬡⬡   BREATHING EXERCISE: [   ]

PRAYER \ MEDITATION \ READING NOTES

NOTES / APPOINTMENTS FOR THE DAY:

Now Plan Your Day ☺

Friday

*But you will not even need to fight. Take your positions; then stand still
and watch the Lord's victory.*
—2 Chronicles 20:17

MORNING ROUTINE

DECREES / AFFIRMATION:

THINGS I AM THANKFUL TO GOD FOR TODAY:

1.
2.
3.

TYPE OF EXERCISE

AMOUNT (DISTANCE, TIME, SETS, REPS, WEIGHT)

CUPS OF WATER: BREATHING EXERCISE:

PRAYER \ MEDITATION \ READING NOTES

NOTES / APPOINTMENTS FOR THE DAY:

Now Plan Your Day ☺

Saturday

Yet in all these things we are more than conquerors through Him who loved us.
—Romans 8:37

MORNING ROUTINE

DECREES / AFFIRMATION:

THINGS I AM THANKFUL TO GOD FOR TODAY:

1. ....
2. ....
3. ....

TYPE OF EXERCISE

AMOUNT (DISTANCE, TIME, SETS, REPS, WEIGHT)

CUPS OF WATER: ⬡⬡⬡⬡⬡⬡⬡⬡   BREATHING EXERCISE: [   ]

PRAYER \ MEDITATION \ READING NOTES

NOTES / APPOINTMENTS FOR THE DAY:

Now Plan Your Day ☺

Date: _____

TO DO BY PRIORITY

- ○ _____
- ○ _____
- ○ _____
- ○ _____
- ○ _____
- ○ _____
- ○ _____
- ○ _____
- ○ _____
- ○ _____

Date: _____

TO DO BY PRIORITY

- ○ _____
- ○ _____
- ○ _____
- ○ _____
- ○ _____
- ○ _____
- ○ _____
- ○ _____
- ○ _____
- ○ _____

Date: _____

TO DO BY PRIORITY

- ○ _____
- ○ _____
- ○ _____
- ○ _____
- ○ _____
- ○ _____
- ○ _____
- ○ _____
- ○ _____
- ○ _____

Date: _____

TO DO BY PRIORITY

- ○ _____
- ○ _____
- ○ _____
- ○ _____
- ○ _____
- ○ _____
- ○ _____
- ○ _____
- ○ _____
- ○ _____

Date: _____

TO DO BY PRIORITY

- ○ _____
- ○ _____
- ○ _____
- ○ _____
- ○ _____
- ○ _____
- ○ _____
- ○ _____
- ○ _____
- ○ _____

Date: _____

TO DO BY PRIORITY

- ○ _____
- ○ _____
- ○ _____
- ○ _____
- ○ _____
- ○ _____
- ○ _____
- ○ _____
- ○ _____
- ○ _____

Date: _____

TO DO BY PRIORITY

- ○ _____
- ○ _____
- ○ _____
- ○ _____
- ○ _____
- ○ _____
- ○ _____
- ○ _____
- ○ _____
- ○ _____

Date: _____

TO DO BY PRIORITY

- ○ _____
- ○ _____
- ○ _____
- ○ _____
- ○ _____
- ○ _____
- ○ _____
- ○ _____
- ○ _____
- ○ _____

NOTES

"Be very careful how you live, not as unwise but as wise, making the most of every opportunity"
- Ephesians 5:15-16

Month:

SUNDAY	MONDAY	TUESDAY	WEDNESDAY

THURSDAY	FRIDAY	SATURDAY	NOTES

Weekly Goal Strategies

Goal Area: . . . .

_____
_____
_____
_____
_____
_____
_____
_____
_____
_____
_____
_____
_____

Goal Area: . . . .

_____
_____
_____
_____
_____
_____
_____
_____
_____
_____

Goal Area: . . . .

_____
_____
_____
_____
_____
_____
_____
_____
_____
_____
_____
_____

Goal Area: . . . .

_____
_____
_____
_____
_____
_____
_____
_____
_____
_____
_____
_____
_____
_____

Weekly Goal Strategies

Goal Area:

_____

Goal Area:

_____

Goal Area:

_____

Goal Area:

_____

Sunday

It is God who arms me with strength,
And makes my way perfect.
——Psalm 18:32

MORNING ROUTINE

DECREES / AFFIRMATION:

THINGS I AM THANKFUL TO GOD FOR TODAY:

1. ....
2. ....
3. ....

TYPE OF EXERCISE

AMOUNT (DISTANCE, TIME, SETS, REPS, WEIGHT)

CUPS OF WATER: ⬡⬡⬡⬡⬡⬡⬡   BREATHING EXERCISE: [＿＿＿]

PRAYER \ MEDITATION \ READING NOTES

NOTES / APPOINTMENTS FOR THE DAY:

Now Plan Your Day

Monday

Arise, shine, for your light has come,
and the glory of the Lord rises upon you.
----Isaiah 60:1

MORNING ROUTINE

DECREES / AFFIRMATION:

THINGS I AM THANKFUL TO GOD FOR TODAY:

1. _____
2. _____
3. _____

TYPE OF EXERCISE

AMOUNT (DISTANCE, TIME, SETS, REPS, WEIGHT)

CUPS OF WATER: 〇〇〇〇〇〇〇〇   BREATHING EXERCISE: [_____]

PRAYER \ MEDITATION \ READING NOTES

NOTES / APPOINTMENTS FOR THE DAY:

Now Plan Your Day

137

Tuesday

The Lord is my light and my salvation; Whom shall I fear?
The Lord is the strength of my life; Of whom shall I be afraid?
——Psalm 27:1

MORNING ROUTINE

DECREES / AFFIRMATION:

THINGS I AM THANKFUL TO GOD FOR TODAY:

1.
2.
3.

TYPE OF EXERCISE

AMOUNT (DISTANCE, TIME, SETS, REPS, WEIGHT)

CUPS OF WATER: ⬡⬡⬡⬡⬡⬡⬡⬡

BREATHING EXERCISE: [   ]

PRAYER \ MEDITATION \ READING NOTES

NOTES / APPOINTMENTS FOR THE DAY:

Now Plan Your Day ☺

Wednesday

You will show me the way of life, granting me the joy of your presence
and the pleasures of living with you forever.
———Psalm 16:11

MORNING ROUTINE

DECREES / AFFIRMATION:

THINGS I AM THANKFUL TO GOD FOR TODAY:

1. ....
2. ....
3. ....

TYPE OF EXERCISE

AMOUNT (DISTANCE, TIME, SETS, REPS, WEIGHT)

CUPS OF WATER: ⬦⬦⬦⬦⬦⬦⬦

BREATHING EXERCISE: ☐

PRAYER \ MEDITATION \ READING NOTES

NOTES / APPOINTMENTS FOR THE DAY:

Now Plan Your Day

Thursday

The Lord is my strength and shield. I trust him with all my heart. He helps me, and my
heart is filled with joy. I burst out in songs of thanksgiving.
——Psalm 28:7

MORNING ROUTINE

DECREES / AFFIRMATION:

THINGS I AM THANKFUL TO GOD FOR TODAY:

1.
2.
3.

TYPE OF EXERCISE

AMOUNT (DISTANCE, TIME, SETS, REPS, WEIGHT)

CUPS OF WATER: 🌢🌢🌢🌢🌢🌢🌢   BREATHING EXERCISE:

PRAYER \ MEDITATION \ READING NOTES

NOTES / APPOINTMENTS FOR THE DAY:

Now Plan Your Day 🙂

Friday

Finally, be strong in the Lord and in his mighty power.
—Ephesians 6:10

MORNING ROUTINE

DECREES / AFFIRMATION:

THINGS I AM THANKFUL TO GOD FOR TODAY:

1. _____
2. _____
3. _____

TYPE OF EXERCISE

AMOUNT (DISTANCE, TIME, SETS, REPS, WEIGHT)

CUPS OF WATER: 🝆🝆🝆🝆🝆🝆🝆   BREATHING EXERCISE: [_____]

PRAYER \ MEDITATION \ READING NOTES

NOTES / APPOINTMENTS FOR THE DAY:

Now Plan Your Day ☺

Saturday

Be still, and know that I am God.
—Proverbs 13:4

MORNING ROUTINE

DECREES / AFFIRMATION:

THINGS I AM THANKFUL TO GOD FOR TODAY:

1.
2.
3.

TYPE OF EXERCISE

AMOUNT (DISTANCE, TIME, SETS, REPS, WEIGHT)

CUPS OF WATER: ⬭⬭⬭⬭⬭⬭⬭   BREATHING EXERCISE:

PRAYER \ MEDITATION \ READING NOTES

NOTES / APPOINTMENTS FOR THE DAY:

Now Plan Your Day ☺

Date: _____

TO DO BY PRIORITY
○ _____
○ _____
○ _____
○ _____
○ _____
○ _____
○ _____
○ _____
○ _____
○ _____

Date: _____

TO DO BY PRIORITY
○ _____
○ _____
○ _____
○ _____
○ _____
○ _____
○ _____
○ _____
○ _____
○ _____

Date: _____

TO DO BY PRIORITY
○ _____
○ _____
○ _____
○ _____
○ _____
○ _____
○ _____
○ _____
○ _____
○ _____

Date: _____

TO DO BY PRIORITY
○ _____
○ _____
○ _____
○ _____
○ _____
○ _____
○ _____
○ _____
○ _____
○ _____

Date: _____

TO DO BY PRIORITY

○ _____
○ _____
○ _____
○ _____
○ _____
○ _____
○ _____
○ _____
○ _____
○ _____

Date: _____

TO DO BY PRIORITY

○ _____
○ _____
○ _____
○ _____
○ _____
○ _____
○ _____
○ _____
○ _____
○ _____

Date: _____

TO DO BY PRIORITY

○ _____
○ _____
○ _____
○ _____
○ _____
○ _____
○ _____
○ _____
○ _____
○ _____

Date: _____

TO DO BY PRIORITY

○ _____
○ _____
○ _____
○ _____
○ _____
○ _____
○ _____
○ _____
○ _____
○ _____

NOTES

"Be very careful how you live, not as unwise but as wise, making the most of every opportunity"
- Ephesians 5:15-16

Weekly Goal Strategies

Goal Area: ....

Goal Area: ....

Goal Area: ....

Goal Area: ....

Weekly Goal Strategies

Goal Area:

Goal Area:

Goal Area:

Goal Area:

Sunday

"Do not be afraid of them, for I am with you and will rescue you,"
declares the LORD.
——Jeremiah 1:8

MORNING ROUTINE

DECREES / AFFIRMATION:

THINGS I AM THANKFUL TO GOD FOR TODAY:

1.
2.
3.

TYPE OF EXERCISE

AMOUNT (DISTANCE, TIME, SETS, REPS, WEIGHT)

CUPS OF WATER: ⬤⬤⬤⬤⬤⬤⬤

BREATHING EXERCISE: [　　　]

PRAYER \ MEDITATION \ READING NOTES

NOTES / APPOINTMENTS FOR THE DAY:

Now Plan Your Day ☺

Monday

Peace I leave with you; my peace I give you. I do not give to you as the world gives.
Do not let your hearts be troubled and do not be afraid.
——John 14:27

MORNING ROUTINE

DECREES / AFFIRMATION:

THINGS I AM THANKFUL TO GOD FOR TODAY:

1. _____
2. _____
3. _____

TYPE OF EXERCISE

AMOUNT (DISTANCE, TIME, SETS, REPS, WEIGHT)

CUPS OF WATER: ⬡⬡⬡⬡⬡⬡⬡   BREATHING EXERCISE: [ ]

PRAYER \ MEDITATION \ READING NOTES

NOTES / APPOINTMENTS FOR THE DAY:

Now Plan Your Day :)

Tuesday

May the God of hope fill you with all joy and peace as you trust in him, so that you may overflow with hope by the power of the Holy Spirit.
—Romans 15:13

MORNING ROUTINE

DECREES / AFFIRMATION:

THINGS I AM THANKFUL TO GOD FOR TODAY:

1.
2.
3.

TYPE OF EXERCISE

AMOUNT (DISTANCE, TIME, SETS, REPS, WEIGHT)

CUPS OF WATER: 〇〇〇〇〇〇〇〇   BREATHING EXERCISE: [   ]

PRAYER \ MEDITATION \ READING NOTES

NOTES / APPOINTMENTS FOR THE DAY:

Now Plan Your Day ☺

Wednesday

For the Lord takes delight in his people; he crowns the humble with victory.
——Psalm 149:4

MORNING ROUTINE

DECREES / AFFIRMATION:

THINGS I AM THANKFUL TO GOD FOR TODAY:

1. _____
2. _____
3. _____

TYPE OF EXERCISE

AMOUNT (DISTANCE, TIME, SETS, REPS, WEIGHT)

CUPS OF WATER: ⬡⬡⬡⬡⬡⬡⬡   BREATHING EXERCISE: [ ]

PRAYER \ MEDITATION \ READING NOTES

NOTES / APPOINTMENTS FOR THE DAY:

Now Plan Your Day 🙂

Thursday

When doubts filled my mind, your comfort gave me renewed hope and cheer.
——Psalm 94:19

MORNING ROUTINE

DECREES / AFFIRMATION:

THINGS I AM THANKFUL TO GOD FOR TODAY:

1.
2.
3.

TYPE OF EXERCISE

AMOUNT (DISTANCE, TIME, SETS, REPS, WEIGHT)

CUPS OF WATER: ⬡⬡⬡⬡⬡⬡⬡   BREATHING EXERCISE: [   ]

PRAYER \ MEDITATION \ READING NOTES

NOTES / APPOINTMENTS FOR THE DAY:

Now Plan Your Day ☺

Friday

He gives power to the weak and strength to the powerless.
—Isaiah 40:29

MORNING ROUTINE

DECREES / AFFIRMATION:

THINGS I AM THANKFUL TO GOD FOR TODAY:

1. ....
2. ....
3. ....

TYPE OF EXERCISE

AMOUNT (DISTANCE, TIME, SETS, REPS, WEIGHT)

CUPS OF WATER: ◊◊◊◊◊◊◊◊   BREATHING EXERCISE: ☐

PRAYER \ MEDITATION \ READING NOTES

NOTES / APPOINTMENTS FOR THE DAY:

Now Plan Your Day ☺

Saturday

These things I have spoken to you so that My joy may be in you, and
that your joy may be made full.
——John 15:11

MORNING ROUTINE

DECREES / AFFIRMATION:

THINGS I AM THANKFUL TO GOD FOR TODAY:

1.
2.
3.

TYPE OF EXERCISE

AMOUNT (DISTANCE, TIME, SETS, REPS, WEIGHT)

CUPS OF WATER: ⬭⬭⬭⬭⬭⬭⬭⬭

BREATHING EXERCISE: [   ]

PRAYER \ MEDITATION \ READING NOTES

NOTES / APPOINTMENTS FOR THE DAY:

Now Plan Your Day

Date: _____

- ○ _____
- ○ _____
- ○ _____
- ○ _____
- ○ _____
- ○ _____
- ○ _____
- ○ _____
- ○ _____
- ○ _____

Date: _____

| TO DO BY PRIORITY |

- ○ _____
- ○ _____
- ○ _____
- ○ _____
- ○ _____
- ○ _____
- ○ _____
- ○ _____
- ○ _____
- ○ _____

Date: _____

| TO DO BY PRIORITY |

- ○ _____
- ○ _____
- ○ _____
- ○ _____
- ○ _____
- ○ _____
- ○ _____
- ○ _____
- ○ _____
- ○ _____

Date: _____

| TO DO BY PRIORITY |

- ○ _____
- ○ _____
- ○ _____
- ○ _____
- ○ _____
- ○ _____
- ○ _____
- ○ _____
- ○ _____
- ○ _____

Date: _____

- ○ _____
- ○ _____
- ○ _____
- ○ _____
- ○ _____
- ○ _____
- ○ _____
- ○ _____
- ○ _____
- ○ _____

Date: _____

TO DO BY PRIORITY

- ○ _____
- ○ _____
- ○ _____
- ○ _____
- ○ _____
- ○ _____
- ○ _____
- ○ _____
- ○ _____
- ○ _____

Date: _____

TO DO BY PRIORITY

- ○ _____
- ○ _____
- ○ _____
- ○ _____
- ○ _____
- ○ _____
- ○ _____
- ○ _____
- ○ _____
- ○ _____

Date: _____

TO DO BY PRIORITY

- ○ _____
- ○ _____
- ○ _____
- ○ _____
- ○ _____
- ○ _____
- ○ _____
- ○ _____
- ○ _____
- ○ _____

NOTES

"Be very careful how you live, not as unwise but as wise, making the most of every
opportunity"
- Ephesians 5:15-16

Weekly Goal Strategies

Goal Area:

Goal Area:

Goal Area:

Goal Area:

Weekly Goal Strategies

Goal Area:

Goal Area:

Goal Area:

Goal Area:

Sunday

*Restore to me the joy of your salvation
and grant me a willing spirit, to sustain me.*
—Psalm 51:12

MORNING ROUTINE

DECREES / AFFIRMATION:

THINGS I AM THANKFUL TO GOD FOR TODAY:

1.
2.
3.

TYPE OF EXERCISE

AMOUNT (DISTANCE, TIME, SETS, REPS, WEIGHT)

CUPS OF WATER: ⬫⬫⬫⬫⬫⬫⬫   BREATHING EXERCISE: ☐

PRAYER \ MEDITATION \ READING NOTES

NOTES / APPOINTMENTS FOR THE DAY:

Now Plan Your Day

Monday

Though you have not seen him, you love him; and even though you do not see him now, you believe in him and are filled with inexpressible and glorious joy.
—1 Peter 1:8

MORNING ROUTINE

DECREES / AFFIRMATION:

THINGS I AM THANKFUL TO GOD FOR TODAY:

1. _____
2. _____
3. _____

TYPE OF EXERCISE

AMOUNT (DISTANCE, TIME, SETS, REPS, WEIGHT)

CUPS OF WATER: ⬡⬡⬡⬡⬡⬡⬡⬡

BREATHING EXERCISE: [   ]

PRAYER \ MEDITATION \ READING NOTES

NOTES / APPOINTMENTS FOR THE DAY:

Now Plan Your Day ☺

Tuesday

You have given me greater joy than those who have abundant harvests of grain
and new wine.
——Psalm 4:7

MORNING ROUTINE

DECREES / AFFIRMATION:

THINGS I AM THANKFUL TO GOD FOR TODAY:

1.
2.
3.

TYPE OF EXERCISE

AMOUNT (DISTANCE, TIME, SETS, REPS, WEIGHT)

CUPS OF WATER: 🌢🌢🌢🌢🌢🌢🌢   BREATHING EXERCISE: [ ]

PRAYER \ MEDITATION \ READING NOTES

NOTES / APPOINTMENTS FOR THE DAY:

Now Plan Your Day 😊

Wednesday

Hear me as I pray, O Lord. Be merciful and answer me! My heart has heard you say, "Come and talk with me." And my heart responds, "Lord, I am coming."
——Psalm 27:7–8

MORNING ROUTINE

DECREES / AFFIRMATION:

THINGS I AM THANKFUL TO GOD FOR TODAY:

1. _____
2. _____
3. _____

TYPE OF EXERCISE

AMOUNT (DISTANCE, TIME, SETS, REPS, WEIGHT)

CUPS OF WATER: ⬡⬡⬡⬡⬡⬡⬡ BREATHING EXERCISE: [＿＿＿]

PRAYER \ MEDITATION \ READING NOTES

NOTES / APPOINTMENTS FOR THE DAY:

Now Plan Your Day ☺

Thursday

For the joy of the Lord is your strength.
——Nehemiah 8:10

MORNING ROUTINE

DECREES / AFFIRMATION:

THINGS I AM THANKFUL TO GOD FOR TODAY:

1. ....
2. ....
3. ....

TYPE OF EXERCISE

AMOUNT (DISTANCE, TIME, SETS, REPS, WEIGHT)

CUPS OF WATER: ⬯⬯⬯⬯⬯⬯⬯⬯   BREATHING EXERCISE: [＿＿＿]

PRAYER \ MEDITATION \ READING NOTES

NOTES / APPOINTMENTS FOR THE DAY:

Now Plan Your Day ☺

Friday

When you go through deep waters I will be with you.
—Isaiah 43:2

MORNING ROUTINE

DECREES / AFFIRMATION:

THINGS I AM THANKFUL TO GOD FOR TODAY:

1. _____
2. _____
3. _____

TYPE OF EXERCISE

AMOUNT (DISTANCE, TIME, SETS, REPS, WEIGHT)

_____   _____

_____   _____

_____   _____

_____   _____

CUPS OF WATER: 🜄🜄🜄🜄🜄🜄🜄   BREATHING EXERCISE: [ ]

PRAYER \ MEDITATION \ READING NOTES

_____
_____
_____
_____
_____
_____
_____

NOTES / APPOINTMENTS FOR THE DAY:

Now Plan Your Day

Saturday

Have I not commanded you? Be strong and courageous. Do not be afraid; do not be discouraged, for the Lord your God will be with you wherever you go.
——Joshua 1:9

MORNING ROUTINE

DECREES / AFFIRMATION:

THINGS I AM THANKFUL TO GOD FOR TODAY:

1.
2.
3.

TYPE OF EXERCISE

AMOUNT (DISTANCE, TIME, SETS, REPS, WEIGHT)

CUPS OF WATER: ⬭⬭⬭⬭⬭⬭⬭⬭

BREATHING EXERCISE:

PRAYER \ MEDITATION \ READING NOTES

NOTES / APPOINTMENTS FOR THE DAY:

Now Plan Your Day

Date: _____

TO DO BY PRIORITY

○ _____
○ _____
○ _____
○ _____
○ _____
○ _____
○ _____
○ _____
○ _____
○ _____

Date: _____

TO DO BY PRIORITY

○ _____
○ _____
○ _____
○ _____
○ _____
○ _____
○ _____
○ _____
○ _____
○ _____

Date: _____

TO DO BY PRIORITY

○ _____
○ _____
○ _____
○ _____
○ _____
○ _____
○ _____
○ _____
○ _____
○ _____

Date: _____

TO DO BY PRIORITY

○ _____
○ _____
○ _____
○ _____
○ _____
○ _____
○ _____
○ _____
○ _____
○ _____

Date: _____

TO DO BY PRIORITY

○ _____
○ _____
○ _____
○ _____
○ _____
○ _____
○ _____
○ _____
○ _____
○ _____

Date: _____

TO DO BY PRIORITY

○ _____
○ _____
○ _____
○ _____
○ _____
○ _____
○ _____
○ _____
○ _____
○ _____

Date: _____

TO DO BY PRIORITY

○ _____
○ _____
○ _____
○ _____
○ _____
○ _____
○ _____
○ _____
○ _____
○ _____

Date: _____

TO DO BY PRIORITY

○ _____
○ _____
○ _____
○ _____
○ _____
○ _____
○ _____
○ _____
○ _____
○ _____

NOTES

"Be very careful how you live, not as unwise but as wise, making the most of every opportunity"
- Ephesians 5:15-16

Weekly Goal Strategies

Goal Area:

Goal Area:

Goal Area:

Goal Area:

Weekly Goal Strategies

Goal Area:

Goal Area:

Goal Area:

Goal Area:

Quarterly Goal Evaluation

o How did I do at working towards my goal this quarter?
o What things should I start doing to reach my goal?
o What things should I stop doing that are holding me back?
o What should I keep doing that has/have been helping?
o Prayer Requests / Answered Prayers

GOAL

GOAL

GOAL

GOAL

Quarterly Goal Evaluation Continued

Let God transform you into a new person by changing the way you think, then you will
learn to know God's will for you which is good and pleasing and perfect.
—Romans 12:2 (NLT)

GOAL

GOAL

GOAL

GOAL

Printed in the United States
by Baker & Taylor Publisher Services